THE
CANADIAN
ENTERTAINERS
OF WORLD WAR II

Ray Stephen

To Maria from
Ed Hall
2288 Fox Cr.
Ottawa ON
Canada
K2B 7K8

RCL Branch 148
Renfrew Ont

Canadian Cataloguing in Publication Data

Stephens, W. Ray (William Ray), 1916-
    The Canadian entertainers of World War II

ISBN 0-88962-529-8 (bound)   ISBN 0-88962-528-X (pbk.)

1. World War, 1939-1945 - Theater and the war.
2. World War, 1939-1945 - Music and the war.
3. Entertainers - Canada. I. Title.

D810.E4S84 1993   940.531579   C93-093406-7

Published by MOSAIC PRESS, P.O. Box 1032 Oakville, Ontario, L6J 5E9, Canada. Offices and warehouse at 1252 Speers Road, Units #1&2, Oakville, Ontario, L6L 5N9, Canada.

Mosaic Press acknowledges the assistance of the Canada Council and the Ontario Arts Council in support of its publishing programme.

Copyright © W. Ray Stephens, 1993
Design by Asterisk Communications
Typeset by Jackie Ernst

Printed and Bound in Canada.
ISBN 0-88962-528-X PAPER   ISBN 0-88962-529-8 CLOTH

MOSAIC PRESS:
In Canada:
    MOSAIC PRESS, 1252 Speers Road, Units 1&2, Oakville, Ontario, L6L 5N9, Canada. P.O. Box 1032, Oakville, Ontario L6J 5E9
In the United States:
    John Calder (Publishers) Ltd., 9-15 Neal Street, London, WCZH 9TU, England.

THE
CANADIAN
ENTERTAINERS
OF WORLD WAR II

W. Ray Stephens CD

MOSAIC PRESS
Oakville-New York-London

TABLE OF CONTENTS

Dedicated to The Stephens' Family

FOREWORD

Moral building was always an essential part of wars.

Where there were warriors, there were also the minstrels.

In Biblical times we read where the trumpets blew down the Walls of Jerico. This action by musicians threatened to alter the course of military strategy and henceforth the bands were put to the rear in order to fight battles with honour, dignity and the usual amount of bloodletting.

There was, and still is, adversity among military circles who feel that the uplifting of moral among troops is non-contributive. Even as far back again as the Biblical times, King David, who was a fair performer himself on the nebel, an early guitar, when celebrating before the Ark of God with noisy timbrels, psalteries, cymbals, trumpets and singers, was severely criticized by Amos (isa.v.12) in that..."Take thou away from me the noise of thy song...Woe to those who chant to the sounds of the nebels..."

And Athelia, one of the local royalty, complained crying "Treason! Treason!" commonly referred to today as 'bloody band!' when King David and his priests 'blew loud noises.' However, Asaph, the highest priest who doubled in execution, had poor Athelia's head cutoff. This met with the approval of the other musical priests including one, Jahazriel, who begat Jazz and played lead trumpet.

Centuries later, in England, glum Oliver Cromwell, took a dim view when he passed... "An Act against vagrants and wandering, idle dissolute persons, commonly called fiddlers, or minstrels and making music...shall at any time after July 1st 1656, be taken playing, fiddling and making music...shall be adjudged as rogues, vagabonds and sturdy beggars and shall be punished accordingly."

And there were those who appreciated the musicians as we read in Orders of the 24th Regiment, The South Wales Borderers: "Bandsmen, being better educated and in a position superior to the rank and file, must remember that more is expected of them. Their conduct should be beyond reproach and in their dress and bearing, they should be the smartest men in the battalion."

Kind words indeed but of little comfort when on January 22, 1897, the two battalions of the regiment were totally destroyed by the Zulus in the one sided battle of Isandhlwana. Among the 1,329 soldiers of the regiments killed were the two regimental bands.

At the outset of the American Civil War, 1862-65, all bands and entertainment were found as non-essential, but a year later, Patrick S. Gilmore, bandmaster of the Boston Infantry Band and formerly a clarinet player from Ireland and the Royal Artillery Band in Montreal, was called upon to form one hundred bands as quickly as he could. Then along came the early concert parties for the troop, in the form of 'family acts.' The Family Hutchinson, The Baker Family, The Blakely Family, The Cheney Family and others including singers, actors and so forth, making the first U.S.O. in American history. Entertainment was in high demand as brother fought brother, and from Switzerland came the Family Ranier, causing the Family Hutchinson to write a song of protest.

When foreigners approach your shore
You welcome them with open doors
Now we have come to seek our lot
Shall native talent be forgot?

Author as Corporal with regiment
(PPCLI) in Cove Barracks, Aldershot,
England. Feb 1940, Age 23.

Irving Berlin formed his World War 1 (1914-1918) show "Yip, Yip, Yaphank" in Camp Upton in 1917, but when World War II (1939-1945) broke out he was refused permission at the very same camp under the assumption that entertainment was not needed.

He persisted and along came his greatest show "This Is The Army" for which he was presented a special medal by the President after the war.

The renowned "Dumbells" made Canada famous in the world of entertainment when they were formed in France in August of 1917. One year earlier the Princess Patricia's Canadian Light Infantry had created their own front line show and they became the nucleus of the Dumbells.

So we come to the outbreak of World War II in September 1939.

Canada had only four permanent force army bands. The Royal Winnipeg, Manitoba, the Royal 22nd in Quebec and the Royal Canadian Horse Artillery in Kingston. These staff bands were instantly disbanded to serve as stretcher bearers or regular soldiers regardless of the fact that by the time the screening was completed no more than 25 able bodied men marched off to war without the ceremony of a band because there were none.

In mid 1941, the second year of the war, the Canadians stalemated in England. The Battle of Britain was won, the enemy invasion had been called off and the need for entertainment, bands, etc. grew urgent.

So began the formation of ten staff army bands of 27 members and the creation of 'soldier concert parties' with all personnel taken from every serving regiment, unit and corps stationed in England at that time.

Thus began the creation of Canada's greatest and most professional entertainment units in all of our history. Bands, concert parties, The Army Shows, Meet the Navy Show, the RCAF bands and others by which for $1.50 per day Canada had the finest material ever assembled and by the end of the war, had produced more professional talent than any time for or ever again.

These are their stories.

Special Acknowledgement

A very special mention of gratitude must be expressed for much of the assistance in research not only from the Archives in Ottawa but also from other sources within this book.

Edward G. Hall, (Eddie), President Emeritus of the Ottawa Musicians' Association, long time friend of the author and lead trumpet in the overseas band of the Royal Canadian Artillery.

Eddie's diligence, perseverance and determination has been truly far beyond the call of duty.

Eddie is shown here as a "boy soldier" in the Royal Canadian Horse Artillery (Kingston, Ontario) at the age of 16 in 1938.

◀

The author and Billy Cobb of the band with Dutch family, Verbeek in Hilversum May 1945, a few weeks after Liberation. Note that uniforms still show signs of winter wear in Italy. ▶

The family Verbeek in 1980 when author visited them. ▶

INTRODUCTION

While attempts have been made to create as expansive as possible, a look back over the years to the story of Canadian Entertainment of World War II, it must be realized that in this, an extremely specialized and forgotten segment of war history, very little was actually documented or recorded due to the fact that bands, concert parties, shows and entertainment in general were seldom considered in the 'warrior' category.

History has shown, however, that the 'minstrels of war' could always be found doing what they did best despite adverse conditions and situations far beyond the normal where the only medals came in the form of applause and appreciation from the thousands of soldiers, sailors and airmen, who found relief and a happy escape from the horrors of war.

Undoubtedly, there are many, many more stories left untold but I wish to thank all of those who did take an interest in this project including the numerous newspapers across Canada who ran my requests free of charge.

W. Ray Stevens CD

WORLD WAR I AND INTERIM

Though the slaughter of World War I (1914-1918) was horrendous, the need for entertainment was never more pressing since that war was fought on a stagnant piece of land for four years.

In June of 1916, there appeared the concert party of the Princess Patricia's, known as the Princess Patricia Comedy Company. It was formed from front line soldiers and they gave excellent shows a few miles behind the lines.

Later, in August of 1917, many of the PPCC joined forces with the newly created Canadian Dumbells, who went on to international fame and even a stint on Broadway after the war ended.

One member (Canadian), Gitz Rice, of the PPCC, who played occasional piano between battles, is credited with the version of "Mademoiselle From Armentieres" as well as many songs of that era including "Keep Your Head Down, Fritzie Boy!" Gitz was badly wounded towards the war's end and was sent back to Canada in 1918.

The Princess Patricia's Comedy Company (1916)

Original cast included Jack McLaren, J.W. Filson, F. Fenwick, C. Stephens, T.J. Lilly, S.C. Nicholls, C. Hillman, N.J. Nicholson Pembroke. (5638 Public Archives)

The Dumbells Created in August of 1917 and included:

Ted Newman (centre), Jack Ayres (kneeling), Jack McLaren (far right), Ross Hamilton (Marjorie far left at 6 ft.), Capt. Al Plunket (director in dress suit), Ted Charters (wig outfit), Jimmy Goode (blackface), Fred Fenwick (female by Jack Ayres), A. Holland, Leonard Young, Bill Tennant, Bert Langley and Elmer Belding.

The Concert Part of the PPCLI (Princess Patricia's Canadian Light Infantry) before the war in 1937, Winnipeg. Author was one of the "harem" girls. (Far right rear) On author's right, Larry Thor, who became Sam Spade in New York radio show "Broadway in My Beat." Other "girls" include Cec Shea, who was killed in Italy in 1944 as was the officer Lt. Foster.

Third from left is Sergeant Major Harper who later became Colonel of the Officer's Training School in England, and, second from left, Drill Sergeant Miller, became Regimental sergeant Major of the same training school.

On extreme right, Sergeant O. Gardner became Regimental sergeant Major overseas, through Korea and after. The other two in the front line also became Sergeant Majors' proving that Sergeant Majors' after all, are very good actors.

CONCERT BAND OF PPCLI, WINNIPEG, 1938.

The breaking up of this first class band in December 1939 saw many of the bandsmen improve their military status.

Clarinet, La Plante, was commissioned as was trombone player, Frank MacDonald, who instructed at the Officers' Training School in England. "Staff" Shawcross, trumpet, became a Major in Korea; Arthur Fraser, French Horn also a Major with Fort Garry Horse tanks; Jack Jackson, went into the Provost Corp. overseas. Bill Moskalyk, bass drum, won a scholarship while in England to study at the Royal Academy of Music, on voice, and was later killed when he rejoined the regiment in Italy.

THE BANDS

General

FORMATION OF THE CANADIAN MILITARY BANDS OVERSEAS

By the End of 1940, the Canadian Army command sought various means of moral support and the first units to be created were the 10 military staff bands consisting of 27 musicians and 1 English bandmaster.

The bands were called upon for every possible type of service. Parades, inspections, church parades, dances, concerts, civilian affairs and were kept busy seven days a week with several performances daily.

Next came the Canadian Soldier Concert Parties and eventually other units sent from Canada.

.....

In early 1941, Former PPCLI bandmaster A.K. Streeter, an Englishman, was posted overseas to form the Canadian Army bands which would eventually total 270 musicians of bandsmen. The members of the displaced regular bands joined first and the first band formed, the 1st Infantry Division, found 18 members of the PPCLI band transferred.

Were bands necessary?

When one considers that there were only ten Canadian bands of 27 musicians each for almost a half million troops overseas the answer is quite obvious.

MARCHANT'S HILL CAMP SCHOOL

First Anniversary Celebrations, 1941

1st Canadian Division band playing for "May Dances" in Surrey 1941. Note varied headdress before bands became uniformed. Shortly after this pleasant scene was taken, the siren went warning of approaching air raid and everyone dispersed to their respective shelters.

9

COUNTY BOROUGH OF EAST HAM.
EDUCATION COMMITTEE.

MARCHANT'S HILL CAMP SCHOOL,
HINDHEAD, SURREY.

SPRING FESTIVAL
PROGRAMME.

WEDNESDAY, JUNE 3rd, 1942,
At 2.15 p.m.,
AT THE HINDHEAD PLAYING FIELDS.

No. 1 Canadian Infantry Band
will be in attendance.

PROCEEDS IN AID OF BRITISH AND RUSSIAN
RED CROSS AND LOCAL CHARITIES.

The early official bands were often "loaned" out to support civilian moral. Factories, clubs, festivals etc. were all added to the daily workload of the bands quite apart from military duties.

In one case, members of the 1st Division band were called upon to assist in the presentation of the masque "Alfred" by Thomas Arne written in 1740 from which "Rule Britannia" appeared.

A Greeting !

"A fellah fra' Bolton
A chap fra' Wigan
A Manchester business man
and a Liverpool Gentleman

will always rise to the occasion at the mention of their "local town Band."

But today CANADA SPEAKS !
Our visitors are indeed radiant messengers of Dominion neighbourliness and family devotion in their Mother country—musicians by intuition, but soldiers through circumstance. Theirs is the true spirit of Empire Fellowship. While this spirit lives in the hearts of men the Bond of Union which unites the Commonwealth of British People will at all times endure.

"The trumpet words of Jefferson
To bugle forth the rights of man."

E.W.

When the first official Canadian band was formed in England in mid 1941 (The 1st Division) it was in great demand not only by the armed forces but also by civilian organizations.

THE SUTTON AND CHEAM BOROUGH COUNCIL
Municipal Open-Air Theatre - Season 1941

A Programme of Music
—BY—
A CANADIAN MILITARY BAND
(By kind permission of Brigadier F. R. PHELAN, D.S.O., M.C., V.D.)

Conductor - Mr. W. GARNETT

...day, September 6th, 1941   at 6.0 p.m

PROGRAMME
"O CANADA"

MEDLEY	"Martial Moments"	Arr. Winter	6	Airs from - "Please, Teacher"	Wall...
	"Nights of Gladness"	Ancliffe	8	MEDLEY "The Gay Nineties"	Arr. Wint...
om -	"The Desert Song"	Romberg	9	WALTZ "Smiles, then Kisses"	Anclif...
	"Fifty Years of Song"	Arr. Ord Hume	10	ENGLISH AIRS - "The Rose"	Arr. Myddlet...
	"Pique Dame"	Suppé	11	MEDLEY OF AMERICAN AIRS -	Arr. Ord Hum...
	"On Grandma's Birthday"	Rathke	12	MARCH MEDLEY "Colonel Bogey on Parade"	Arr. Alfo...

INTERVAL   GOD SAVE THE KING

10

Band of the 1st Canadian Division playing from balcony in San Vita, Italy. Jan. 11, 1944, (PA 150925 Photo by Terry F. Rowe)

Canadian band playing for the Princess Louise ▲ Dragoon Guards and Royal Canadian Engineers. San Vito, Italy. April 2, 1944 (PA 152149 Photo by A.M. Stirton)

Band of 4th Canadian Infantry Division ▲ playing down main street for liberation of Rouen, France. Sept. 12, 1944 (PA 152142 Sgt. Million)

Band of the 1st Canadian Infantry Division playing for patients in hospital are at San Vita Chietino, Italy, January 12, 1944. (PA 152161 Photo by A.M. Stirto)

Among the many duties of the bands, was the follow up burial services for the fallen Canadians. This meant the playing of The Last Post by band members.

In the case of the above (below) band, this was the duty of L.Cpl. Johnny Doeg, seen in Picture on side drum. Johnny, or the Guardsman as he was known for his military bearing, was perhaps one of the finest trumpeter for military calls.

Another excellent bugler was Sgt. ''Jack'' Mackie of the PPCLI. In December of 1943, the aftermath of the vicious battle for Ortona, left the 2nd Brigade almost wiped out. The PPVCI, the Loyal Edmonotans and the West Nova Scotias, were able to group only a few hundred survivors from what was the most costly conflict of the war in Italy.

''I knew it was my job to lay the Last Post for the PPCLI as the remnants gathered on a rain soaked hillside outside of Ortona and when I stepped forward to do my duty, I was faced by Sgt. Jock Mackie, red eyed and battle fatigued. He said that this was his territory and if I didn't mind, he would play the Last Post. I can never forget that moment. No one has ever blown it the way MacKie did. When it was over he stood there crying. We all felt that way.''

Johnny Doeg, Toronto

▼

2nd Canadian Division band at Memorial Service at Lake Superior Regiment. Hengelo, Holland. June 17, 1945 (PA 152152 Photo by B.J. Gloster)

Canadian mass bands on Dam Square, ▲ Amsterdam playing for parade held for Queen Wilhelmin's return to Holland from Canada. June 28, 1945. *Note band front line of 18 tubas. Troops are the Free Netherlanders. (PA 174332 Photo by B.J. Gloster)

◄

Massed bands in Amsterdam for Queen Wilhelmin's return. June 28, 1945 (PA 166393 Photo by B.J. Gloster)

Band of the 2nd Canadian Infantry Division. Liberation Parade.
Rotterdam. June 1945.
Band about to wheel into position facing saluting stand to march troops past.

Field Days were always needed to keep the troops occupied. This one where the Band of the 1st Canadian Infantry Division played appropriate ''sports music'' on July 27th 1942 for the 2nd Canadian Division was indeed the end of whole Canadian division for on August 19, 1942, just over two weeks later, the Canadians attacked and were horribly massacred in the infamous Dieppe disaster. Included were many militia ex-bandsmen who had been posted to first aid positions as stretcher bearers.

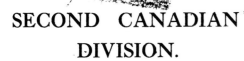

SECOND CANADIAN DIVISION.

Major-General J. H. ROBERTS, M.C.,
Divisional Commander.

TRACK & FIELD
and
TUG-OF-WAR
CHAMPIONSHIPS

27th July, 1942.

Competing Groups :	Group Colours
R.C.A. 2 CDN. DIVISION	Black
4 CDN. INF. BDE. GROUP	Green
5 CDN. INF. BDE. GROUP	Red
6 CDN. INF. BDE. GROUP	Blue
DIVISIONAL TROOPS GROUP	Gold

CANADIAN ARMY, ENGLAND.

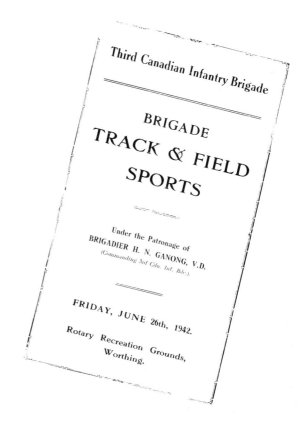

Third Canadian Infantry Brigade

BRIGADE
TRACK & FIELD SPORTS

Under the Patronage of
BRIGADIER H. N. GANONG, V.D.
(Commanding 3rd Cdn. Inf. Bde.)

FRIDAY, JUNE 26th, 1942.

Rotary Recreation Grounds, Worthing.

FIRST CANADIAN DIVISION

Track
and
Field
Championships

Major-General G. R. Pearkes,
V.C., D.S.O., M.C.,
General Officer Commanding

JULY 1st, 1942

Bands 1 ▲
Band of the 1st Canadian Infantry Division, formed in mid-1941, chiefly from ex-bandsmen of the Princess Patricia's Canadian Light Infantry peace time band. Bandmaster W.O. Buckmaster (Cheshire Regiment) was the first of the British bandmasters on loan to the Canadian Army. Author, as band sergeant, is extreme left on tuba.

Band 10 ▲
Band of the 3rd Canadian Infantry Division behind GENERAL CRERAR as they received the Polish General K. SOSKISKI, England, May 25, 1944
Photo by Michael Dean

Band of the 2nd Canadian Infantry Division playing concert in field in Italy, May 28, 1944 Note audience of two boys and a dog. One boy is wearing Canadian Army boots.
(PA 152146 Photo by C.E Nye)

MISCELLANEOUS ▲
#19 Unit CANADIAN ARMY SHOW. (picture from Norm Foster, Sarnia, Ont.)
Girls: Margarite Smith, Ann Richardson, Marie Foster, Marian Gerdung, Jackie Nickerson, Joyce Cork, Gingie Arnett

#19 Unit CANADIAN ARMY SHOW (picture from Norm Foster, Sarnia, Ont.)
Girls in front row: Joan Godfrey, Joyce Cork, Marie Foster, Jean Stewart, Ann Richardson. *Girls in rear*: Jackie Nickerson, Patti and Kitty Smith. Leader was W.O. 1 Jack Kane. (Centre of girls front row) Based in Guildford, Surrey, England, 1944

14

Navy Bands
H.M.C.S. AVALON (Photo from Norm Foster, Sarnia, Ont.)
Members include: Don Echford, Slim Clifford, Ed Curry, McKay, Charles and George Browning, Bob Haberer, Roy Schafer, Vic Welby, R. Patterson, R. Ingles, D. Reid, A. Moorees, Guy Noakes (Bandmaster), etc.

NAVY BANDS
H.M.C.S. ONTARIO (Picture from Norm Foster, Sarnia, Ont.) ▼

RCA BAND 16
Liberation parade in Hilversum, Holland, May 1945

Same location, 1985. Picture taken by Eddie Hall, (Ottawa)

Canadian Bandmaster, W.O. 1 Phil Murphy (Windsor, Ont.) conducts the Canadian Armoured Corp. Band in Arnhem, April 19, 1945, two days after the city fell to heavy fighting. Note the haggard faces of the children behind the bandmaster.
(PA 159565 Photo by Jack Smith)

Tin Hats
PA 152146 Lt. Gilroy of the Tin Hats Review.
Italy, April 15, 1944 Photo by Barry Gilroy

▲ PA 152127 Tin Hats in Ottawa, January 3,
1945 before returning to Europe after
regrouping. Glen Morley at piano.

Bandoliers serenading horse in Germany.
March 8, 1945. Bill Gerber (trumpet) C.
Richards on accordion
        (PA 174313 Photo by Donald Grant)

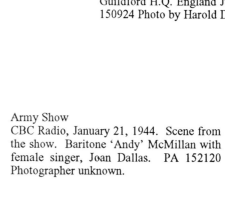

The Army Show.
Senior CWAC officer Lt. Verity Sweeny
(later married to Lt/Col Rai Purdy) assists
with Alice blue gown of singer Mary Leonard.
Guildford H.Q. England June 21, 1945 (PA
150924 Photo by Harold D. Robinson)

Army Show
CBC Radio, January 21, 1944. Scene from
the show. Baritone 'Andy' McMillan with
female singer, Joan Dallas. PA 152120
Photographer unknown.

The Army Show
Singer Pte Paul Carpenter. Army Show
Broadcast. London, England June 29, 1945.
(PA 152137 Photo by Harold D. Robinson)

Brass section of Army Show orchestra.
London, England June 29, 1945. Trumpets
include Fred David and George Anderson
and trombones Teddy Roderman and Murray
Ginsberg. (PA 152132 Photo by Harold D.
Robinson)

Unit of Army Show in Italy May 14, 1944.
Tenor Roger Doucet and baritone, Andy
McMillan entertain Canadian Paratroopers.
(PA 152145 Photo by D.A. Reynolds)

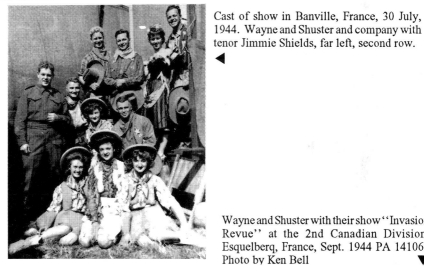

Cast of show in Banville, France, 30 July,
1944. Wayne and Shuster and company with
tenor Jimmie Shields, far left, second row.
◀

Wayne and Shuster with their show "Invasion
Revue" at the 2nd Canadian Division.
Esquelberq, France, Sept. 1944 PA 141069
Photo by Ken Bell ▼

Invasion Revue
Wayne and Shuster (Johnny and Frank) in
German outfit by German road sign. Bergues,
France Sept. 16, 1944. PA 137316 Photo by
Ken Bell ▼

WAYNE &
SHUSTER

17

French civilians gather near Canadian soldiers for Invasion Revue, Banville, France, July 30, 1944. PA 141068 Photo by Ken Bell.

The happy accordion trio of Les Foster, Billy Mae Dinsmore and Dixie Dean. (PA 174272 Photo by Richard Arless) Aug. 27, 1943.

◀ *Rhythm Rodeo*
Private Pat James astride her favourite mount 'Smoky' chatting with 'Indian' Private Chick Cole. Pepper Harrow. England, December 16, 1945 (PA 174329 ?)

The famous team of Allan and Blanche Lund (then Harris) (PA 174267 Photo by Richard Arless) Aug. 27, 1943.

Meet the Navy Show
John Pratt and his memorable showstopper "You'll Get Used to It" Aug, 1943 (PA 174268 Photo by R. Arless)

Three elaborately gowned women (CWAC) make an impressive tableau in the finale of the show. Pepper Harrow. England, December 16, 1945 PA 176428 Photo by Arthur Cole

◀ Cpt. Andy Jamieson curries horse before show. Pepper Harrow. Dec. 16, 1945 (PA 174334 ?)

A trio of the same beauties from the W. Debs.
RCAF: LAW Lenore Barlow, Cpl Celeste
Smith and LAW Doris Bouvette (PL 24700
DND)

A bevy of beauties from the all RCAF girl
show "W. Debs" dancing the Can-Can at the
RCAF Repatriation Depot in Torquay,
England, 1945. Left to right: Cpt Celeste
Smith (Winnipeg) LAW Doris George
(Toronto) LAW Lenore Barlow (Vancouver)
LAW Nonnie Stockton and LAW Doris
Bouvette. (PL 45017 DND)

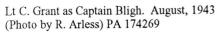

Lt C. Grant as Captain Bligh. August, 1943
(Photo by R. Arless) PA 174269

Stage Door Canteen, London, England
Scene from the Gay '90s with RCAF LAW
Florence Allen and LAC S. Alman. (PL 46235
DND)

19

DANCE
To Canadian Rhythm

OZZIE LEWIS
AND HIS
TEN RED FLASHES

Admission 1/6

This was a hand made poster by the Dance Band of the 1st Division. All monies went to the purchase of suitable dance band equipment and music. The army didn't issue such equipment.

ROYAL CANADIAN ARMY SERVICE CORPS

FIRST CANADIAN ARMY TROOPS

TUG - OF - WAR, BASEBALL, TRACK & FIELD CHAMPIONSHIPS

20 SEPT. 42

THE ROYAL CANADIAN ARTILLERY BAND

(Overseas 1942-45)

After serving with the 1st Infantry Division band from 1941, the author was transferred to the newly formed Royal Canadian Artillery Band in 1943. The first book *The Harps of War* (1986) gives a detailed history of this artillery band from its early beginning in England, the broadcasting duties in London, the winter of 1944 in Italy and then France, Belgium, Holland and Germany.

By the time this band was formed from overseas personnel, it became more difficult to get even 27 musicians to fill the gaps. The English bandmaster came from the British 3rd Hussars while there were representatives of the four pre-war bands, the Royal Canadian Regiment (1), the Princess Patricia's Canadian Light Infantry (1), the Royal 22nd Regiment (1) and the Royal Canadian Horse Artillery (3). Others came from the Canadian Provost Corps (1), the 1st Canadian Paratroop Battalion (1), Canadian Armoured Corp (1), Canadian Grenadier Guards (1), Seaforth Highlanders of Canada (1), Heavy Anti Aircraft (1), Light Anti Aircraft (1), Priests (1) and one older member who had served in the American submarine service in World War 1.

▲ Band of the Royal Canadian Artillery combined with an American band playing for U.S./Canadian athletic meet in England. April 22, 1943

Band master W.I.1 R.A. Newman (Royal Canadian Artillery) conducting
Note: Americans wearing greatcoats. Canadians, more accustomed to English dampness, are in battle dress only. Also, Americans used sousaphones while Canadians had upright tubas.

► The early band in the spring of 1943. Camp Bordon, England.

► The complete band, late 1943. Camp Bordon, England.

Ready for full parade and duties. Camp Bordon, England, 1943

First formation of the dance band.

Rear row: Hall, McCaskill, Chandler, Gibson, Stephens
Front row: Perry, Hayter, Thomson, Cobb

Combined band unit with members of the Canadian Grenadier Guards Band, later to become the band of the 2nd Canadian Infantry Division, 1943.

MEMORANDUM
23/BROADCASTS.1/2
49/GEN/ADAG(B)

20th June 1944

BROADCASTS A.E.F. (Allied Expeditionary Forces Network)
CANADIAN BANDS

The DDPR has requested...that the RCA (Royal Canadian Artillery) Band...be retained in U.K. for the purpose of providing radio programmes for the AEFP...This band was selected some weeks ago to proceed to Italy.

Major Meredith...urges very strongly that the RCA band...is essential to the Canadian contribution...of the highest calibre...They (band) have had considerable experience in broadcasting...However, the RCA band has been briefed and prepared to proceed to the Mediterranean Theatre (North Africa and Italy) and...it would be considered ''detrimental to their morale to cancel their services overseas at this late date...''

(However)...

The band suffered their sorrows in not going to Italy at that time and went to London to work for several months on radio. *Monday Night Variety Show* with guests such as Margaret Eaves, Tessie O'Shea, Audrey Pullen, Joyce Grenfell, Alex Pleon, Vic Oliver, Olive McGee, Al Moddy Etc.

Tuesday Dance Band Programme
Wednesday Concert Programme
Thursday Bea Lillie Nightcap
Friday Ranch House Party
Saturday Johnny Canuck Review
Sunday Rehearsal for next week's shows

During that four month period, Hitler, released some 5,000 v1's or Buzz Bombs on London.

Notes from the Official Diary of the RCA (Royal Canadian Artillery) Band

16 July 1944
...returning to London...carried all equipment for some 300 yards past Surbiton Station to another train...Buzz bomb destroyed station...

25 July 1944
...to Broadcasting House for recording...air attacks getting worse...used deep down Security Studio.

29 July 1944
Bandsman, T. Nutt, was married this afternoon to Rose Pither of Lyons Place, London...Ceremony interrupted several times by falling Buzz Bombs...one hitting a five story building near by...Nutt was reported as saying...''I've heard of shotgun weddings but this is ridiculous!''

30 July 1944
Rehearsal and recording at Fortune Theatre cancelled due to technical difficulties...(It had been partially destroyed by a Buzz Bomb!)

OFFICIAL ORDERS
29 SEPTEMBER 1944

Royal Canadian Artillery Band, London
The Entertainment Unit under Robert Garnon has now arrived from Canada...for AEFF Broadcasting...
The Royal Canadian Artillery Band can now be despatched to Italy on the next convoy.

MAYOR'S PARLOUS, TOWN HALL WINBLEDOM

Officer Commanding Canadian H.Q. London
25th October 1944

Royal Canadian Artillery Band
...could we retain the services of your famous RCA band...
                    Reed Daniel, Mayor

(Reply)

3RD NOVEMBER 1944

Band no longer in the United Kingdom...
                    P.J. Montague, Maj. General, Administration

THURSDAY, FEBRUARY 15, 1945

Band in stopover at Fabrianno after crossing the Appennines with the Canadian Corps headed for Europe. Left Ravenna February 13 and arrived France March 3, 1945. Welch, Watkins, Tanner, Perry, Hutchinson, Royle with front, Chandler, Thomson, Hayter.

Dance band set up for outdoor music. Nijmegan, March 1945.

Saxes: Cob (Newcastle, NB); Herbert (Kitchener, ON); Thomson (Moosejaw, Sask.); Hayter (Stratford, ON)
Brass: Chandler (Vancouver, BC); Hall (Kingston, ON); McCaskill (Montreal, PQ); Watts (Manitoba)
Rhythm: Stephens (Bass, Winnipeg, Man.); Watkins (drums, Hamilton, ON); Perry (piano, PEI); Hutchinson (guitar, Vancouver, BC)
Banners were hand made by Larry Tanner (Ottawa), drummer in the band.
Bandmaster: R.A. Newman ▼

MARCH 1945

First stop from Italy. Pub in Merkham, Flanders where band billeted for a while, Author inside doorway; Chandler with pup; Watkins; unknown; Georgo (driver); unknown Flemish lass; Cobb (with his spaghetti style winter wear). Front row: Hayter; Welch.

Dance band playing by roadside in Germany ▲ for Troops.

Jack Hayter, Saxophone didn't like anyone reading over his shoulder. Nijmegan, March 1945. (Band members were all issued by 9 mm revolvers) ▶

24

One of the "bridges too far" over the Rhine.

Repossessing piano from house in KLEIVE, Germany. April 1945 Soldier with axe is piano tuner and player, Joe Perry.

The combined band of the Royal Canadian Artillery and the Canadian Armoured Corp (54 musicians) play alternately for over four hours non stop for the march past of the complete 3rd Canadian Division in Utrech, Holland on June 6th, 1945.

Less than a month after "V.E. Day" the Canadian regiments paraded in preparation for their "victorious" return home, however, troops were not exactly "warriors." Within few weeks of the war's ending, all veterans were quickly sent home unheralded.

During the parade, in which every regimental and unit march was properly played, the side drummer of the Armoured Corp band broke a drum head which meant that the Artillery side drummer (Tanner) had to play for almost two hours without missing a single beat. "I couldn't lift by arms for days" Tanner from Ottawa related.

25

Going home after six years. Band departing Calais, France for England, September 1945. But it was not the end. They returned again to Europe.

And so the curtain closes.

Last extracts from the diary of The Royal Canadian Artillery Band. All entries ended with weather report.

6th August 1945
Bandmaster R.A. Newman admitted to hospital in U.K.

21st November 1945
...band lost six veterans...weather bright.

22nd November 1945
...band warned for haircuts. weather bright.

23rd November 1945
...Dance band truck fell into canal...weather cloudy and cool.

21st December 1945
...nothing much...5th Armoured Division breaks up...weather cool, cloudy

7th February 1946
...despatched to 1st Canadian Depot...weather fair.

15th February 1946
...Final disbandment...This is the last diary entry of The Royal Canadian Artillery Band Overseas...weather cloudy with rain.

THE ROYAL CANADIAN ORDNANCE CORP BAND

RUSS KEARNS, SURREY, BC

RCOC Band playing on beachhead shortly after "D" Day June 1944. St. Aubin sur Mer., France

▲ Concert in Tilburg, Germany

▲ Dance band in Ghent, Belgium, 1944

Washing day somewhere in France. Photo by Russ Kearns

Trumpet trio from the RCOC band formed on board Queen Elizabeth going overseas. Herb Dowding, Russ Kearns and Bill White. Photo Russ Kearns ▶

ROYAL CANADIAN ARMOURED CORP BAND

DIARY EXTRACT FROM AUTHOR'S BOOK THE HARPS OF WAR, 1986

Diary entry, April 19, 1945

"Yesterday in Germany, today back in Holland.

We moved into Arnhem where we met with some of the band of the Canadian Armoured Corp. Arnhem fell two days ago after very heavy artillery shelling and house to house fighting. Only buildings left are on the edge of the town where dazed civilians are walking around and starving.

The army has set up a mess tent across the road from where we are billeted in an old house but one look at the frightened and hungry people lining up for leftover scraps is enough to turn one off even army grub.

The mess sergeant shouts "IF you want seconds you bloody well better eat it!"

They open the kitchen to the hungry lined up with their little pails and pans. These are not beggars but middle class folks searching for scraps not for themselves, for their children.

After the first few meals, the line up has grown blocks long. The local police are called into disperse them. We feed the police.

What the hell is a band doing here when everyone is starving to death? All I can think about is that being in a band following a war is like being in a band following a parade of horses. No matter how carefully one treads, sooner or later you're bound to step in the shit.

"Note: During the next few months over 150,000 Dutch people, mostly the elderly and the very young, died of starvation.

Band of the Canadian Armoured Corp in Bijmegen, Holland, April 9th, 1945, one month before "V.E. Day" and the liberation of the rest of Holland by the Canadians.
Note the war torn but happy faces of the youngsters who are also wearing Canadian battle dress and berets, some even this regimental badges. Also little girl holding Union Jack and Stars and Stripes. (PA 170301 Photo by Jack Smith)

Canadian Armoured Corp Band in Arnhem, April 19, 1945
The first taste of liberation by the Dutch. (PA 134483 Photo by Jack Smith)

Band sergeant P. (Pete) Graham. Canadian Armoured Corp band demonstrated xylophone to two Dutch boys in Bijmegen, Holland. April 9, 1945. Note: Canadian army fatigue tunics on boys as well as army boots and web belt. (PA 17035 Photo by Jack H. Smith)

THE SOLDIER CONCERT PARTIES

The Tin Hats

After the bands began their formation in mid 1941, the 'soldier concert parties' came into being later on that year:

"They were formed by Captain F. Anders of the Canadian Legion in co-operation with the Red Cross, Knights of Columbus and the Salvation Army. We were the first show formed (in England), due mostly to our great comedian, Wally Brennan. He was the show's director. We first followed the tradition of the famous World War I Canadian Dumbells and since we had no attached females we too adapted by the use of female impersonators.

We toured Africa and Italy and then returned to England where shortly after "D" Day (June 6, 144) on our way across the English Channel to France, we were torpedoed with a loss of 5 men from our show. (See Soldier Party Documentation for details)

We then joined the Canadian Army Show and I remember cute Lois Maxwell, the Moneypenny later of the James Bond movies and her friend, Gwen Dainty, very well.

Later we were sent back to Canada for some more touring and time to rebuild and then, after V.E. Day, went back to Europe once more."

Bill Dunstan, Ottawa, Ont.

'TIN HATS' REVUE SENSATION WITH CANADIANS OVERSEA

Toronto Entertainers Help Make Show Success—Perform at Ambassadors

BATTLE-DRESS BOYS

Somewhere In England, Dec. 19—(CP) — A rollicking, tuneful, musical revue called "Tin Hats" has made a sensational hit in the Canadian army camps.

These battle-dress troupers played twice through the Canadian corps to large soldier audiences

"We became the first official concert party overseas and began giving shows in September 1941. On October 9th, 1941, we gave our first big show at the Ambassadors Theatre in London, England. I was with various groups before joining the Tin Hats and in late 1940, worked with Stan Sheddon (Sgt) of the 49th Edmonton Regiment, in creating a show at the Hammersmith Palais in London called Maple Leaf Matinee, later known as Johnny Canuck Review."

Glen Morley, Vancouver, BC

The orchestra and cast of the first Canadian all-soldier musical revue, the Tin Hats, in the finale of their show at London's Ambassadors Theatre, 9 October 1941. (DHist, DND, 5043)

Front row:
Ronnie White, Johnny Heawood, Wally Brennan, Joe Rocks, Bill Dunstan, Spud Cooper
Band:
Charlie More (trumpet, killed when torpedoed); Eric Halsall; Les Abrums (drums); Harry Connolly and Stan Stevenson (saxes); Bert Churchill (piano)

TIN HATS
PA 152148 Left to Right:
Private Bill, Dunstant; Supervisors W.J. Gagnon, J.M. O'Reagan; F.J. Flanagan; J.W.C. Tierneu; Lt. J.B. Hay; Private J.E. Heawodd and Major W. "Scotty" McLaws.
Italy, April 12, 1944
▼   Photo by G. Barry Gilroy

The Tin Hats on Harlequin. September 3, 1943. PA 150926 Photo by C.E. Bud Nye

Tin Hats back in Canada January 1945 before return again to Europe.

Army Troupe Returns To Canada

AFTER six months' trouping, the Canadian Army show "Tin Hats" has returned home to put together a new production for the front line overseas circuit. Torpedoed en route to France, they lost four of the cast. Of the 22 who survived, six were wounded. They plan to have a short leave before regrouping and when the new show is completed, will move to the Northwest European Front to play as they did in Africa and Italy. Left above, Pte R. White, Grand Falls, N.B., looks over the shoulders of feminine impersonators Pte. Bill Dunstan, Regina, and Pte. John Heawood, Toronto, as they make up. Right: Cowboy crooner Pte. M. E. Harper, with his mandolin. All members are ex-combatant soldiers.

CASUALTIES OF WAR
On July 26, 1944, the Soldier Concert Party of the Tin Hats, while en-route by a navy craft to France from England, were torpedoed with a loss of five members of the group.

For documented details see official report under "Documents".

The Kit Bags

Programme of Kit Bags at Scotland's Garrison Theatre, Edinburgh for Sunday 14th June 1942 from Ron Gates, Burlington, Ont.

Pictures and information from Terrence Spencer, Medicine Hat, Alberta.

See also "Soldiers Concert Parties" for further details.

"...there were five concert parties in the Soldier Concert Party establishment...TIN HATS. KITBAGS. BANDOLIERS. FORAGE CAPS and HAVERSACKS. The Haversacks being last formed did not have a very long life, likewise the Forage Caps."

Terrence Spencer. Medicine Hat, Alberta

Lou "Pops" Hopper leading. They were soon absorbed into the regular army show and back into uniform. ▶

North of Rome, September 1944. ▲
Our first ration of beer on the road up at lunch time. Note the old Italian woman. She got a kick out of having her picture taken.
Terrence Spencer,
Medicine Hat, Alberta

Programme from 1942

October 1944. Italy, Grand Hotel, Riccione. This was the big R and R, for the Canadians just south of the battle line (winter 1944) of The Rivers around Ravenna. I was admitted to hospital before this picture was taken. (Terrence Spencer)

THE HIGH CONSTABLES OF EDINBURGH
present

SCOTLAND'S
GARRISON
THEATRE
CLERK STREET   EDINBURGH
NEW VICTORIA

Every Sunday at 7.30 p.m. prompt

A Bright Musical Show with Smart Dancing and Snappy Comedy for the Uniformed Services of the Allies

Programme

Sunday, 14th June 1942

104th Week

TERRENCE SPENCER

A few memories.

Edmonton October 23, 1939

Letter to Terrence

Dear Sir:

We are organizing a band for the 49th Edmonton Regiment for overseas service and we have a vacancy for trombone.

...Fred Hobson mentioned you...If you are interested in enlisting please let me know...

W. Ernest Berry, Cpl 15634
Edmonton Regiment Band

The newly outfitted band of the Edmonton Regiment leads the parade prior to leaving for overseas in December 1939.

To Terrence from Fred Hobson

Dear Terrence:

Got your letter yesterday...glad you joined up...I figure it is better to be in the band while there's a chance of...foot slogging...It's the life of Riley. $1.30 a day and everything all found except beer and cigarettes...We never get up before six a.m. ....and then practice at nine...We have 18 in the band now...and need a good trombone like you...Stan Shedden is band sergeant and a hell of a good guy...We practice a lot of Gilbert and Sullivan because it is the colonel's favourite stuff.

I figure...when we get out we'll be pretty good musicians...Go down to Eastern Canada for a good musician job...But in here we can get forty bucks a month clear...

Yours, Fred.

SO TERRENCE JOINS.

In December 1939, the Edmonton Regiment went overseas with the 2nd Brigade alongside the Princess Patricia's Canadian Light Infantry. While the militia unit of the Edmonton's were given new instruments for their band, the permanent force PPCLI band was disbanded.

In Farnborough, England, their band was reduced considerably but with some ex band members of the PPVCI, who borrowed enough instruments to cover their needs, a fair sized camp band was formed to play concerts in the NAAFI.

In 1943, Spencer went to the "Bandoliers" after a stint or so with other groups including the "Kit Bags." They left for Italy in August 1944 but in October, he caught yellow Jaundice and eventually shipped back to England, although during a stay over at Gibraltar, the convoy was heavily attacked by submarines. The Bandoliers included an all male cast with impersonators, fire eater, dancers and singers.

Terrence Spencer is presented with a new trombone from the City of Edmonton before going overseas with regiment.

One of the Programmes featuring Canadian dance bands in England (Brighton) in 1940 etc.

WINTER GARDENS PAVILION

DANCE TO
THE FAMOUS CANADIAN

MAPLE LEAF'S
BROADCASTING DANCE BAND

featuring BILL CHRISTMAS Canada's Ace Trumpeter   MAURICE TAYLOR Canada's
Golden Voiced Baritone   JESS VAN HOCKEM Canada's Accordian   ERNIE HOLDEN &
CHICK ZANIC Two Funny Fellows and JACK DAVIES Canada's Singing Compere

TUESDAY Dec. 8th	POLICE BALL	7.30 to 12.0
WEDNESDAY Dec. 9th	GIRLS TRAINING CORPS. YOUTH BALL	8.0 to 12
FRIDAY Dec. 11th.	POPULAR DANCE	7.30 to 11.0
SATURDAY Dec. 12th.	POPULAR DANCE	7.30 to 11.0

TEA DANCES
WEDNESDAY AND SATURDAY at 3.15

Table Seats may be Reserved at the Winter Gardens Pavilion Box Office

The B Andoliers dance band.

October 18, 1944. Italy, Mud, mud and more mud!

The Bandoliers in Cattolica. Italy. September 1944. Adriatic behind them.

Canadian rest centre. Grande Albergo Hotel. Riccione, Italy.

Military notice to Germany citizens posted on notice boards in towns and cities. Also in German.

BANDOLIERS (NOT IN ORDER)
Harold Jackson (drums); Albert King (bass); Bill Graham (trumpet); "Steve" Stevenson; Griffin (sax); Vic Turland (trumpet); G. 'Red' Nicol (trumpet); John Somers (stage manager); Bill Caswell (lights); "Pee Wee" Beaudain (fire eater); Lou "Pops" Hooper (leader); A.S. Gorguin (Electrician); A. Scott (Vocal); Harold Tayler (vocal); S. Ginsberg (piano); Terrence Spencer (trombone).

NOTICE
to Civilians

1. You are now under Military Government.
2. The Allied Troops have come to overthrow Nazi Rule, dissolve the Nazi Party, and abolish the cruel, oppressive and discriminatory laws and institutions which the Party has created.
3. Courts and educational institutions are suspended.
4. All officials will remain at their posts until further orders and obey the orders of the Military Government.
5. All persons engaged in essential work will remain at their work.
6. Espionage, sabotage, communication or attempt at communication with the German armed forces, armed attack or armed resistance to the Allied Forces, or assault on any member of the Allied Forces may be punished by death.
7. Firearms, including sporting guns other lethal weapons, ammunition, explosives, wireless transmitters, signalling equipement, and carrier pigeons must be surrendered immediately.
8. All persons will at all times carry their national identity cards.
9. Complete blackout will be observed from sunset to sunrise.
10. All persons are forbidden to be out of doors from sunset until sunrise.
11. Immediately on receipt on this order, everyone must remain indoors for 24 hrs. After 24 hrs. have elapsed, female persons only may be out of doors between the hours of 10 a.m. and 11 a.m., 3 p.m. and 4 p.m. in order to attend to essential household duties.
12. Civilians will NOT be permitted on roads except when bearing an official pass issued by Military Government only. Military Government will give further instructions.
13. The householder or his representative must put up a list on the door of each house of all persons at present occupying the house giving surname, christian name, date of birth. This list must be exhibited within 1 hour of receipt of this order.
14. Anyone who possesses any of the following: MUNITIONS, EXPLOSIVES, CAMERAS BINOCULARS, or any form of apparatus for transmission of information, including Wireless Sets and Carrier Pigeons, must prepare an inventory there of and affix it to the door of his house. Members of the Volksturm are not exempted from his Order. Offences against this Order can be punished by death.
15. The foregoing is only a summary of some of the principal laws and orders of the Military Government. The relevant enactments are posted up in full in all towns and larger villages. It is your duty to make yourselves familiair with them and from now on you will be deemed to have knowledge of their contents.

Forage Caps

The Forage Caps was the fifth Soldier Concert Party formed overseas following the TIN HATS (1941), HAVERSACKS, KITBAGS, and BANDOLIERS.

Later several other groups were created such as RAPID FIRE, OFF THE RECORD, ABOUT TURN, ETC. but it was late 1944.

One of the veteran performers was BILL PAUL;
"I was married with three children when I joined up and I still had three children when I came back. I went overseas in December 1940 with the Royal Canadian Horse Artillery and the moment we arrived in Aldershot, England, I joined a unit concert party then they picked the ones they wanted to form the Concert Parties (Soldier Concert Parties) and our group became known as THE FORAGE CAPS. I played drums and minstrel bones, sand and tap danced. They called me "Doc Bones" and I then went on to direct several other travelling army shows including HILL BILLY BLUES and RHYTHM RANCH BOYS. Our groups were right out in the field living in the same manner as the men they entertained. I went through Italy, France, Belgium, Holland and Germany. Most of our original unit came from Smith Falls. In Italy, I ran across a friend of mine, Don Smith who came back stage one time all covered in mud. IN later life he became Judge D.C. Smith."

Bill Paul, Smith Falls.

The 'Forage Caps,' shown here on stage in Italy 1944, performed in the field, usually just a short distance from the front lines.

Smith Falls Record News. November 8, 1989

Always entertaining

Even between shows, Bill Paul (holding sword) and his 'Hill Billy Blues band could be found performing. Here, he knights a fellow showman.

The Forage Caps, with Bill Paul as a bearded old hillbilly, performed throughout Europe. This picture was taken in England, in 1943.

Les Abrum, Brockville, Ontario

(Taped interview with Eddie Hall of Ottawa, 1989)

"I ended with the Forage Caps, but went through quite a bit of other entertainment before...My work became that of director and producer...rather than drummer. I played at the Hammersmith in London on Maple Leaf Matinee with guys like Stan Sheddan, who came from the Edmonton Regiment as sergeant and ran the show, and Bert Churchill, another Edmonton, was on piano. Glen Morley was also with it but he did most of the arranging etc. ...later the show became Johnny Canuck's Review...I got to know Rai Purdy well. He was in charge of the Army Show...I remember Bert Witherall very well and did he ever have a great hand for scroll writing? Best ever...I was with the Tin Hats along with More on trumpet...he was killed along with Witherall and some others when they got torpedoed in the English Channel.

We went to London to do a radio show for the Allied Radio network and we had to sing a song like "We're over here for the second time"...meaning World War I but Wally Brennan, the great comedian and I put new lyrics to it at the rehearsal but they threw it out and almost us as well...

Les Abrum

"We're over here for the second time
With some B... S... for the C.B.C.
We just hope it's the last time
Just a few jokes for you and me
So roll out the strip
Get set for the job
But when folks hear, they'll say 'corn on the cob'
Oh, we're over here for the second time
With some B... S... for the C.B.C.
    Oh Gerry Wilmot...
With some B... S... for the C.B.C. ..."
.....

I worked with Lou (Pops) Hopper for a while in his Royal Canadian Artillery Concert Party...later the R.C.A. band took most of the guys like Jimmy Thomson, Billy Cobb, McCaskill, and that crazy drummer, Wilkie...he played with Peterson after the war.

I'm now 80 going on 81, so can look back with gratitude for that war time experiences...When war broke out in 1939, I got mixed up in directing a show with some of the World War I Dumbells...Al Plunket; Red Newman; Jack Ayres and Ross Hamilton. Roly Young of the Glove and Mail put it together but we did a week or so at the Royal Alex and it folded... (Chip Up Review)...Nobody wanted that World War I stuff...and it was rough watching those old guys trying to buy a little more time down memory lane."
Les Abrums.

Hold Your Hat

HOLD YOUR HAT REVIEW

Produced by Lt. Steve Nickling of Hamilton, Ontario (in sailor suit)
Groningen, Holland.   October 5, 1945.
PA174331 Photo by Angelo R.H.C.

Ted Keane Stratford, Ontario
"I covered Canada, the Aleutian Islands and overseas in World War II...We had the Canadian Fusiliers Band until it was broken up and made into the Royal Canadian Ordinancy band in England...but I was transferred over to the concert party "Hold Your Hat" under Steve Nickling...Roy McLeod was our first bandmaster and he became one of the first Canadian bandmasters overseas under Streeter...Murphy was the first.

I ended up in the Rhythm Rodeo under Lt.Col. Rai Purdy in Guildford, Surrey...we called it "Guild for Gulch"...

In Canada, our regiment went to Seebee, Alberta in 1943 to escort and chain the German prisoners of war...We got away from that deal fast...but one time in Otter Lake, B.C. our band tent burned from an overheated wood stove and we lost a lot of instruments but what was even worse was the fact that we all carried 30 rounds of .303 ammo plus two hand grandes a piece so when they blew all hell broke loose...

We had to dress in G.I. American uniforms when we went to the Aleutian Islands and then we invade Kiska with the U.S. troops...

In England...we went one Christmas Eve to play carols in Godalming, not far from Guildford and after a few hours of no response we broke out into some New Orleans type stuff...

This sent the mayor over the top...he screamed that "...for over one hundred years of tradition...you bloody Canadians have destroy it...!'' At least they took notice then.

I had an interesting experience when I went before Streeter (Director of Bands Overseas) for an audition...who told me that "All Canadian musicians should be milking cows and not playing musical instruments...When I left him some time later I said it was because "I had some cows to milk..." That's when I went to the Army Shows...
Ted Keane, Stratford.

THE ARMY SHOW

Actual programme of original Canadian Army Show, 1943. Supplied by Mrs. Helen Dillon of Toronto (Sgt. Helen Gill). Containing many autographs. Note Louis Hooker, now Moneypenny or Lois Maxwell.

Inside picture with Wayne and Shuster, Lois Maxwell (bottom right corner) in South American costume.
Singer Jimmie Shields, top right hand corner.
Inside programme with autographs.

CBC Radio, Ottawa. January 21, 1944.
"Army Show" under conductor Frank Fusco.
(PA 15215 Photographer unknown)

January 21, 1944. CBC Radio. "The Army
Show" and chorus, Ottawa. Geoffrey
Waddington (or Frank Fusco) conducting.
Jimmie Shields far left with knee upraised.
PA 152116 Photographer unknown

Members of The Army Show in Recording
Session. London, England. June 29, 1945.
Photo by Harold D. Robinson PA 15533

Singer Pte. Joan Dallas at Broadcast. London, England. June 29, 1945 PA152133 Photo by Harold D. Robinson

Gerry Wilmot, CBC war correspondent and Master of Ceremonies for Army Show broadcasts. London, England, June 29, 1945 PA 152140 Photo by Harold D. Robinson

Major Brian Meredith, Radio Officer recording part of Army show. London, England, June 29, 1945. (PA 155535. Photo by Harold D. Robinson) ◄

Capt. ''Bob'' Garnon, conducting the radio orchestra. London, England. June 1945. PA 154625 Photo by Harold D. Robinson ◄

String section of the show during broadcast. London, England. June 29, 1945 (PA 152131 Photo by Harold D. Robinson)

Unit of Army Show. England April 7, 1944
(PA 152157 Photo by Hynes)

Unit of Army Show. England Apri 17, 1944.
(PA 152158 Photo by W.J. Hynes)

THE ARMY SHOW ENGLAND, APRIL 8, 1944

This is ''B'' unit band of the Canadian Army Show overseas. The big ''Army'' show created in Canada, broke up into smaller units, A,B,C,D and E when in England. (With special thanks for details to Eddie Hall (Ottawa) and Jimmy Coxson (Toronto)

Back Row: Lloyd Cook (Bass)

Middle Row: Red Roderman (Trombone); Pete Samborsky (Trumpet); Babe Newman (Trumpet); Mike Barten (Trump/Viola); P. Overhold (Drums); Jim Coxson (Piano)

First Row: Ed Sanborn (Conductor); Lou Sherman (1st Violin); Frank Hosek (Violin); Hank Rosati (Tenor Sax); Moe Weinzweig (Alto Sax); Vic Bott (Tenor Sax)
PA 152150 Photo by Hynes

Canadian Army Show Unit crew members at the Production Centre (Guildford, England) Shows are produced here and created to entertain the troops on the Continent and Britain, chiefly at this period, the Occupation Forces and others awaiting return to Canada.

Clockwise from left.
CSM Anthony Braden (Vancouver); Major Rai Purdy (Toronto) (Head of Army Shows and later Lt. Colonel); CMS Bill Harding (Toronto); Sgt. Helen Gill (Toronto); Lt. Verity Sweeney (Vancouver); CSM Jimmy Hazack (Toronto).
Guildford, Surrey, England June 21, 1945
PA 176438 Photo by Harold D. Robinson

CSM Anthony Braden (Vancouver) head of the music department and his assistant, CPL Ted Ciaschini (Sault Ste. Marie). Guildford, England. June 21, 1945 PA 176441 Photo by Harold D. Robinson

Sgt. Helen Gill (Toronto) wardrobe mistress and dress designer, CPL George St. John Simpson, formerly with the MontrealRepertory Theatre. Guildford, England. June 21, 1945. AP176440 Photo by Harold D. Robinson.

Assistant Producer Lt. Eddy Sanborn (Montreal) reviewing script with Sgt. Doug Romaine (Toronto). Note: "buckteeth" stage propworn by Romaine. (He is the son of Don Romaine, a performer with the World War I Canadian troupe, The Dumbells. June 21, 1945. PA 176439 Photo by Harold D. Robinson

---

NOTE: THE FOLLOWING ARE REMARKS AND COMMENTS FROM ENTERTAINERS WHO WERE THERE.

FROM LOIS MAXWELL (MONEYPENNY)

"...all of us left for Britain and arrived Dec. 23, 1943. The lovely French Canadian singer in one picture, sitting on the far right is a dear friend of mine, Raymond Miranda. I haven't heard from her since 1944.

We arrived in England and were broken up into five units. I was assigned to Unit "D" with comedian, Doug Romaine. Prior to that I was a "gag" girl for Wayne and Shuster...I was 16 and really naive...I still see Gwen Dainty. (Page 28 of your Memories and Melodies book) and she was sent to Italy in late 1944 (with Doucet and McMillan)...then they found out my age and sent me packing but I sent A.W.O.L. and ended up at the Royal Academy of Dramatic Arts where I won the Lady Louis Mountbatten Scholarship..."

Lois Maxwell

GORDON MCLEAN (VICTORIA, BC)

"When I joined the army in World War II, I went into the Canadian Army Show in Canada.

Then, in England, I accompanied tenor Jimmie Shields on tour with the show and also just the two of us.

A popular war song entitled "March To Victory" was written and used in the finale of our show in Canada. I wrote the music and Margaret Toohey (Winnipeg) wrote the words. ▶

I gave 467 single shows in as many camps and theatres in England, Italy, Belgium, Holland and Germany during the 1943-45 period of the war when I served with "D" Unit of the Army Show.

The last performance I took part in was "Rhythm Rodeo" just south of London, England with comedian Doug Romaine. They were great years, never to be forgotten, even now as I approach my 82nd year (1989).

Jack Groob was an excellent violinist with our show as well."

Gordon McLean

JOHN CAVALL, QUEBEC

"Before the war I was known as the "french" singer Jean Cavall and sang on the American Network, NBC, although I was born in Quebec.

I joined the RCAF in Canada as an entertainer but qualified as a fighter pilot on Spitfires in the Far East.

After my tour of duties, I wasposted in Bournemouth, England as entertainment officer and in 1944, I appeared as a singer with the Canadian Army show in London with Bob Farnon and others..."

Jean Cavall

A SOLDIER REMEMBERS

"The Canadian Army show (Unit) took place about May 24th or 25th, 1944 right after we broke the Hitler Line...at a great cost...Thousands of troops gathered on a hillside to see the show...It was outstanding and a surprise...I never heard a word since...There was a man from Montreal (Roger Doucet) who sang "Who Threw the Overalls in Mrs. Murphies Chowder?"

Thomas W. McKenzie, Moose Jaw

From the Canadian Army Newspaper, the Maple Leaf, June 2, 1944 "Meet Private Mary Moyhihan of the Canadian Army Show now touring Italy...May is shown giving out with a new number and judging from the "out-of-this-world" expressions of the soldiers, it must be right up there on the hit parade."

Bob Cringan of the Rhythm Rodeo, leading the band in rehearsal. Canadian Army Show, Guilford, England, June 21, 1945.

"The number of shows you wrote about were "Army Shows". We had a big unit and it was about 1200 strong towards the end. Lt. Col. Purdy was in command.

I enclose a rough chart of the formation as I remember them."

Bob Cringan,
Meaford. Ontario

MURRAY GINSBERG, TORONTO

"I was 19 when I joined the army in 1942 and after training at Barriefield, near Kingston, I played in the depot ordnance band.

In December 1942, I was transferred to the newly formed Army Show under Geoffrey Waddington...Wayne and Shuster were there and so was Jimmie Shields and Bob Farnon. We open our first show at the old Victoria Theatre in Toronto...a band unheard of in those days...4 trombones, 4 trumpets etc., with Babe Newman as lead.

We also had a guy named Pete S.. who often as not forgot the codas...We hadto play for a big deal in Detroit...BIG...The place was filled with top brass from all the Allies and if a bomb had gone off in there, the war would have ended because all the leaders would be missing...Anyway, we played the Stars Spangled Banner in the key of G, on the reverse side it was the key of Ab, you know of course what happened. Pete played the whole thing in the key of Ab, one semitone higher than the rest of us and Geoff (Waddington) went nuts trying to catch his attention but Pete just kept on blowing. Then we played for the Big Quebec meeting with Churchill, Roosevelt and Stalin.

In December they broke up the show into units, A, B, C, D, and E, and went overseas. I was in Unit "A" with Cute Lois Maxwell, who was only about 16, she later became MoneyPenny in the James Bond Movies, she was a real neat chick.

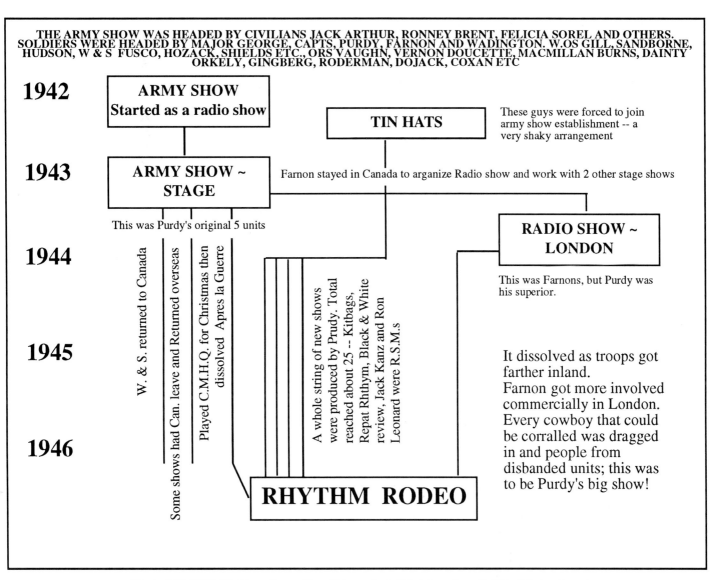

THE ARMY SHOW WAS HEADED BY CIVILIANS JACK ARTHUR, RONNEY BRENT, FELICIA SOREL AND OTHERS. SOLDIERS WERE HEADED BY MAJOR GEORGE, CAPTS, PURDY, FARNON AND WADINGTON. W.OS GILL, SANDBORNE, HUDSON, W & S FUSCO, HOZACK, SHIELDS ETC., ORS VAUGHN, VERNON DOUCETTE, MACMILLAN BURNS, DAINTY ORKELY, GINGBERG, RODERMAN, DOJACK, COXAN ETC

1942 — ARMY SHOW Started as a radio show

TIN HATS — These guys were forced to join army show establishment -- a very shaky arrangement

1943 — ARMY SHOW ~ STAGE — Farnon stayed in Canada to arganize Radio show and work with 2 other stage shows

This was Purdy's original 5 units

1944 — RADIO SHOW ~ LONDON

This was Farnons, but Purdy was his superior.

W. & S. returned to Canada

Some shows had Can. leave and Returned overseas

Played C.M.H.Q. for Christmas then dissolved Apres la Guerre

A whole string of new shows were produced by Prudy. Total reached about 25 -- Kitbags, Repat Rhthym, Black & White review, Jack Kanz and Ron Leonard were R.S.M.s

1945

It dissolved as troops got farther inland. Farnon got more involved commercially in London. Every cowboy that could be corralled was dragged in and people from disbanded units; this was to be Purdy's big show!

1946

RHYTHM RODEO

(Chart by BOB CRINGAN, of Army Show and Repat Rhthym and retired Music Supervisor or Earl Haig Collegiate, Toronto)

Some weeks after "D" Day invasion we went to France and saw the bloody mess of Caen and Falase where the 43rd Canadian Division took it on the chin but got through anyway...then back to England where I joined Lt.Col Rai Purdy and his "Rhythm Rodeo" show. It was a real big show...cowboys, Indians, chuck wagons and the whole mess all under a massive circus tent out in a big field on some estate.

They had to bring in horses from Ireland which was alright but the moment the show opened and the horses entered the tent, they froze under the floodlights and noise...all of them...The only thing that moved was their rear end which kept the poop scoopers busy...

I remember when back in Antwerp, my friend Jack Madden and I, were walking down a street leading to the glass covered railway station when suddenly, out of nowhere, one of the V 2's, the 3000 mile an hour German rocket, hit the station...Glass bricks and everything but we didn't get hurt, however we were so stunned that when our heads cleared a bit we found ourselves several blocks away walking in the wrong direction..."

We had a guy named "Cokey" Campbell who stuttered and one time back in London we were inspected by King George after a show. He (the King) stuttered real bad...But who did he stop to chat with? Cokey of couse.

King: "H..h..h..how are y..y..you?"
Cokey" "F..f..fine s..s..sir."

Murray Ginsberg, Toronto

Rhythm Rodeo

Although the war had now ended, the work of the entertainers still went on.

In perhaps what was a most enterprising venture of The Army Show under the command of Lt/Col Rai Purdy, a mammoth show to be known as "Rhythm Rodeo" was formed on an English estate under a massive circus tent and it drew on the talents of the past six years of war from every segment of Canadian entertainment available. Bronco busters, trick riding and roping and every aspect of the 'old west' including top musicians, dancers, carpenters, electricians and the like, brought together for one last time and effort of the Canadian entertainers overseas.

"Not since the Army Show blazed its way across Canada and The Navy Show (Meet the Navy) played to capacity audiences in London, etc., has any service show received so much attention:
Lt/Col. Rai Purdy.

THE MAPLE LEAF soldier newspaper predicted that the show would surpass both the Army Show and Meet the Navy.

The show opened December 15, 1945 for 2,000 servicemen and women and performed nightly from Monday to Friday. The place of performance was pepper Harrow.

The orchestra numbered 32 musicians under the leadership of CSM Tony Braden with such top grade musicians as Teddy Roderman, Murrey Ginsberg, M. Weinsweig, Murrey Lauder, Chris Lovett, Jimmy Coxon, and others.

Forty lovely girls made up the chorus line and other female acts, while 22 male dancers completed the line up. There were 18 additional tumblers and comedy acts plus 45 cowboys, Indians, drivers, etc. and the stage crew numbered 32.

It was indeed a very big show and by far the largest ever assembled by Canadians during the war.

Vari-coloured curtains for water scenes, revolving stage and elevators that rose to stage level were all part of the production.

It lasted for two and a half hours and the finale alone took 45 minutes when Lt/Col 'Kit'' Carson, a well known Western Canadian rodeo personality, directed 70 horses and riders in an example of the Calgary Stampede.

"I had just left for home in November, 1945 when they were preparing for the big show "Rhythm Rodeo" under Lt/Col Purdy. When I went to CAEU (Canadian Army Entertainment Unit) in March, 1944 it was company strength but was later enlarged to battalion or regimental size and Purdy was promoted from major to Lt/Col. there were two main shows "APRES LA GUERRE" and "RHYTHM RODEO". I remember Jimmie Shields wearing his 48th Regimental shoulder flashes. While working as a stage constructor I made a set of bongo drums for Tony Braden."

Ray Lehman, Troy, Ont.

"I am a former member of the CWAC who was with the Entertainment Units overseas. I was in two shows - "REPAT RYTHM" and "RHYTHM RODEO". The rehearsal for "REPAT RYTHM" was in Toronto then went overseas with approximately 35 members. We travelled all across Europe and England after V.E. Day and then returned to England to join the extravaganza called "RHYTHM RODEO", at a place called Pepper Harrow.

It was quite a show.

They tell me that there is footage of our show in London and in Ottawa."

Bernice Taylor (nee Bridgeman), Simcoe, Ont.

Rhythm Rodeo
Lt Col.Henry (Kit) Carson (Maple Creek, Sask.) at the opening of the Rhythm Rodeo at Pepper Harrow, England, December 16, 1945.
PA 176431 Photo by Arthur Cole

Bucking bronco rider, PRIVATE ANGUS
MACDONALD (Edmonton) tries out a new
mount 'Candy', a baby Shetland pony standing
16" high. Pepper Harrow, England, December
16, 1945 PA 176429 Photo by Arthur Cole

PROGRAMME

RHYTHM RODEO

THE MAPLE LEAF

FOR CANADIAN FORCES IN BRITAIN

Free to Canadian Service Personnel   LONDON, ENGLAND, FRIDAY, OCTOBER 26, 1945   Vol. 1, No. 133

"Rhythm Rodeo" Production Has Something For Everybody—And Horses, Too

They're Shooting The Works On New Army Show

By RUSS STEWART
(Staff Writer)

On a pleasant English estate, not far from Canadian Repatriation Headquarters at Aldershot, the most colorful service show ever conceived, "Rhythm Rodeo" by name, is under production. This new and lavish extravaganza, if colorful costuming, brilliant and original music, plus a unique and strikingly different idea mean anything, threatens to "out-Billy" Billy Rose's Diamond Horseshoe with Aquacade thrown in to boot.

Bronco-busting, trick riding and roping, stage coach hold-ups, in fact a complete Western rodeo, will combine with a musical comedy revue designed to entertain service personnel exclusively. Opening night is set for December 15 and 2,000 servicemen will see each nightly performance, Monday to Friday inclusive.

All tricks of the trade have been thrown in including a vari-colored water curtain for scene changing, a revolving stage, and elevators that rise to stage level. Scores of Army Show personnel are at work fashioning elaborate gowns, cowboy and Indian suits. Under the direction of Sgt.-Maj. Tony Braden, formerly with Mart Kenney's band, background music and original song hits are being whipped into shape and a 32 piece band is in rehearsal.

While carpenters build unusual stage props and electricians harness 250,000 watts for lighting effects, the Army Show's choreographer, CWAC Capt. Verity Sweeney of Vancouver is moulding her girls into smooth choruses ranging from old time square dances to the ballet.

A broad touch of the West will occupy 45 minutes of the two hour show when Lt.-Col. "Kit" Carson, well known in Western Canadian rodeo circles, directs 70 horses and riders in an action-packed, if miniature, version of the Calgary Stampede.

"Not since The Army Show blazed it's way across Canada and the Navy Show played to capacity audiences in London has any service show received such close attention," stated Lt.-Col. Rai Purdy, well known in Canadian radio circles, who will produce and direct "Rhythm Rodeo." "We are confident that we have hit upon an idea that will appeal to all servicemen and women. Every minute of "Rhythm Rodeo" is different . . . ranging from comedy and vivid action to sheer beauty of costuming, lighting and over-all production. As good as were The Army and Navy Shows we sincerely believe that 'Rhythm Rodeo' will be much better."

45

INVASION REVIEW

Unit "D" of the Army Show was later called "Invasion Review" because it landed in France shortly after "D" Day June 6, 1944. Frank Shuster and Johnny Wayne were the stars of this show, along with a very pretty young sixteen year old Canadian, Lois Hooker who became known throughout the world as Moneypenny, of the James Bond series and as Lois Maxwell.

In 1943, Wayne and Shuster had headlined the Army Show on the C.B.C. radio network in Canada under the musical direction of Robert (Bob) Farnon. This radio show also included tenor Jimmie Shields among many others.

Wayne joked upon joining the army, "Things were terribly strict. Lights out at 9 pm and women out at 10." Veteran Robert E. Rae, Toronto writes.

"I served in the Queen's Own Rifles of Canada (Toronto) and went ashore on the beaches of Normandy (Juno) on "D" Day, June 6, 1944, and after weeks of terrible fighting we were drawn back from the front line into reserve for relief and rest on June 27th. The camp was near Cairon, located on a ridge that contained a large cave which was converted into a theatre for performance by a Canadian concert party. (Invasion Review) The show exceeded all expectations. What a wonderful experience we had as Canadian men and women performed for us. Wayne and Shuster were hilarious and Jimmie Shields' beautiful tenor voice, singing all those Irish airs brought tears to our eyes. What a wonderful escape from the tragedy of battles."

The Cave

Did Frank Shuster remember The Cave?

"REMEMBER THE CAVE? We spent eight days in there doing three shows a day for the poor fighting guys! They came in absolutely exhausted. The Canadians had a rough time after the "D" Day landing especially around Caen. We had no choice but to do show after show non-stop and on top of all that I had dysentery, also non-stop. I remember that cave only too well."

Frank Shuster, Toronto
(Wayne & Shuster)

In the picture PA 13839, Wayne and Shuster are shown sitting on the edge of a platform with two lovely Canadian girls behind them. The girl on the right is Enid Powell. "Enid passed away several years ago. Her married name was Powell. I understand that there was some film footage of that show and..while..our family has numerous photos, newspaper articles and (memorabilia) we would love to see some of the film..."
Brian Jenkins, Mississauga, Ont.

Playing for 2nd Canadian Division, Esquelbecq. France Sept. 17, 1944 PA 152141 Photo by Ken Bell.

Girls in Western finale. Banville, France July 27, 1944. PA 132837 Photo by Ken Bell

JOHNNY CANUCK REVIEW

A popular wartime Canadian show on Saturday nights over the B.B.C. radio network and as part of the Allied Expeditionary Forces Network.

It grew from The Soldiers Concert Parties under the name of THE MAPLE LEAF MATINEE from the ever favourite dance hall, The Hammersmith Palais in London.

This original show was co-produced by SGT STAN SHEDDEN, of the 49th Loyal Edmonton Regimental band and GLEN MORLEY from the early Tin Hats. Members included pianist BERT CHURCHILL and HARRY LEEK. "I later transferred to the 1st Canadian Paratroop Battalion in England and was badly wounded in Italy. It was also known for a while as "Western Canadiana" and Billy Christmas, brother of actor Eric Christmas, played lead trumpet."

HAROLD LEEK, Barrie, Ont.

In June 1944, the Royal Canadian Artillery Band took over the first duties for several months when it became "Johnny Canuck's Review" and were later replaced when BOB FARNON arrived from Canada with a selected orchestra that included FRED DAVIS on trumpet. *See also Royal Canadian Artillery Band.

Artists included announcer War Correspondent, GERRY WILMOT, singer EDMUND (TED) HOCKRIDGE, (RCAF) Piano duo, KEN BRAY and NEIL CHOTEM (RCAF) singers, GERRY TRAVERS, PAUL CARPENTER and others.

Certain programmes also included quest bands from the RCAF and other services.

PASS IN REVIEW

"This was not one of the army soldier shows in as much as it was formed from the Canadian Army Show by Robert (Bob) Farnon and Romney Brent. This was my bunch. We toured Canada then went to England as part of the Rai Purdy show, then to Italy, France, Belgium, Holland and Germany.

Romney Brent was a buddy of Cole Porter and co-author of "Nymph Errant". He was a civilian working with the early army shows in Canada.
Robert (Bob) Cringan, Meaford, Ont.

Dean M. Dailey Sarnia, Ont.

"I joined the Canadian army in 1942 and after a year in the ranks I was transferred to the Army Shows on alto saxophone and we toured Canada.

Then over to England but only long enough to say 'hello' before being shipped to Italy with a small group called "OFF THE RECORD".

We spent Christmas of 1944 near the front line in a small Italian village named Godo, just outside Ravenna which was the headquarters of the 5th Canadian Armoured Division under General Hoffmeister, who as just 34 years old at that time.

While the final battle took place within hearing (The Battle of the Rivers) we entertained in a small theatre in the town. We now had four members of the C.W.A.C. (Canadian Womens' Army Corp.) with us but they were stationed in Ravenna.

I remember doing a show for the Van Doo's (Royal 22nd Regiment) that lasted for hours and hours and all the time we were rocked by heavy artillery fire from close by. The Van Doos' would not let us quit and we were completely exhausted and the four girls ended up dancing with the soldiers until early in the morning.

Then we went to France via Leghorn and into Belgium, Holland and Germany. After "V.E.." Day we went back to England and just missed being on the "RHYTHM RODEO" and were sent over to Europe again with a new name "ABOUT TURN" which became "PASS IN REVIEW" with BOB CRINGAN in charge and on alto sax. Later we went back to England but again returned to Europe for the second time. I arrived home in Canada on New Year's Eve 1946.

Coincident
Picture taken in 1944 of DEAN DAILEY and KEN PARKS in the lobby of the Grand Hotel in Riccione, Italy which was the Salvation Army's R and R (Rest and Recreation) base for Canadians. For a pack of cigarettes, an Italian photographer took pictures, first on the war damaged seat shown with Dailey and later on a newer one as seen below with author and friends.

The author, right with friend MURRAY CHURCH, ex PPCLI and now with the R.C.A.S.C. band had this picture taken shortly after Dailey and his friend. When we sat down to have the picture taken, a girl from the CWAC's quickly sat between us and left just as promptly when it was finished. Forty-five years later, through Dean Dailey, she was identified as a member of the troupe Pass in Review and by the name of Garson, however, no one is sure, so the mystery continues.

Dance band of "PASS IN REVIEW" #18 Detachment. Canadian Army Show, Amsterdam, 1945)

Back Row: "Professor" Swetland - Trombone (Montreal); Ray Meunier - Trumpet (Montreal); Gus Degagne - Trumpet (Montreal); Leo Villeneuve - Trumpet (Cornwall); Paul Ayotte - Bass (Montreal); Nick Korn - Drums (Toronto)

Front Row: "The Dean" Dailey - Sax (Sarnia); Bill Johnston - Sax (Victoria); Bob Redmond - Sax (Montreal); Bob Cringan - Sax and leader (Toronto); Gord McLean - Piano (Winnipeg)

THE ROYAL CANADIAN NAVY

MEET THE NAVY

THE ROYAL CANADIAN NAVY

PRESENTS

"Meet the Navy"

PRODUCED BY
THE DIRECTORATE OF SPECIAL SERVICES

Programme of "Meet the Navy Show"
(Cannon) George Young, Oakville, Ont.

Perhaps the greatest show of all times, particularly during the war. Although Irving Berlin's "This Is the Army" has been considered the greatest, the Canadian production far out passed it for quality and professionalism.

"The Royal Canadian Navy Music Review was produced under the supervision of Captain Joseph P. Connelly, director of Special Services for the R.C.N. Rehearsals began in June 1943 in Hart House, University of Toronto. The production staff and company were recognized (somewhat after the fact) by a Government of Canada Treasury Board order in council, August 13, 1943 as "...an establishment to be known as THE NAVY SHOW for the entertainment of Naval, Army and Air Force personnel on active service, and the promotion of recruiting and maintenance of public moral and goodwill..."

It was to be known as "MEET THE NAVY" and due to apparent lack of Canadian leadership skill, a Hollywood producer, Louis Silver and a Broadway choreographer, Larry Ceballos, were brought in to direct and produce the show.

The show premiered for servicemen on September 2nd 1943 at the Toronto Victoria Theatre and opened to the public on September 4th. It played in Ottawa on September 15th at the Capitol Theatre. During the year long Canadian tour, the show covered some 10,000 miles and entertained about one half million Canadians.

In 1944, it went to Britain and opened October 23rd in Glasgow and then toured England, Wales and Northern Ireland. From February 1st to April 7th, they performed at the London Hippodrome including a Command Performance February 28, 1945.

With the fall of Europe, the show went to the continent and gave sellout performances at the Paris Theatre Marigny, The Brussels Music Hall and the Carre Theatre in Amsterdam.

In 1945 the National Film Board of Canada produced a short film entitled "MEET THE NAVY" which has some remarkable segments amid poorly edited film including one of the great basses, OSCR NATZKE, singing an unforgettable "Shenandoah".

Plans for a Broadway run fell through but the show was made into a movie of the same name by Elstree Studio in London, England.

Chorus line of the Meet The Navy Show.
1943 (Photo G.T. Richardson)

The girls of the show. Ottawa August 27,
1943 before departing for overseas. (Photo
by R.G. Arless) PA 152138.

Beverly Baxter wrote in the London Evening Standard:

"Why is this piece so exhilarating, so completely satisfying and, since the first class always touches the emotions, why was it so stirring? Perhaps the answer is that quite outside the professional slickness and the terrific pace of the whole thing, we were seeing the story of Canada unconsciously unfolding itself to our eyes."

Extract from "MEET THE NAVY"
by Ruth Phillips, 1973.

Although today some of the members of the cast frown upon the British made movie, which really should be released from the underground coffers of the Public Archives, it does nevertheless offer moments of great value as to what could be achieved by Canadians even though due to the adversity of war.

The movie is so completely apart from what one would generally associate with a 'service show' and the songs would certainly have remained alive in memory at least if given the exposure of international reviews as did the many surviving songs from England and America. "Meet the Navy" "In Your Little Chapeau" "Beauty on Duty" "Boys in The Bell Bottom Trousers" and of course the show stopper "You'll Get Used To It" as sung by John Pratt plus a fine national song "Canada".

Eric Wild conducted the orchestra and Robert Russell Bennett arranged most of the musical scores. Among the many others who assisted and took leading parts were JOHN PRATT, ROBERT GOODIER, CAMERON GRANT, LIONEL MERTON, ALAN LUND, BLANCHE HARRIS (LUND), OSCAR NATZKE, DIXIE DEAN, BILLY MAE DINSMORE, LES FOSTER, O. HUSTON (Nephew of actor Walter Huston), IVAN ROMANOFF, VICTOR FELDBRILL, GEORGE YOUNG, BILL RICHARDS, CARL TAPSCOTT, etc.

Writers were such as P. QUINN, R.W. HARWOOD, ROY LOCKLEY, W. STEVENS.

A very special thanks to (CANON) GEORGE YOUNG of Oakville who was one of the cast and M.C. for the programme, the notes, information on the films as well as the tales from the

still effervescent BILLY MAE RICHARDS (DINSMORE) plus
ELMER PHILLIPS AND CARL TAPSCOTT.
(*Note Author has a video of the Elstree film and the C.N.F.B.
one. Thanks to Canon Young)

It is also interesting to note that many Canadian shows,
particularly the civilian ones were sponsored and supplied by
private companies. In the case of Meet The Navy, the costumes
were supplied by T. Eatons, the Robert Simpson Co. Ltd., and
the Canadian Celanese Ltd. Danzian's famous New York
theatrical accessories sent many necessary requirements and the
House of Hollywood and Max Factor Inc. presented every
member with individual make up kits.

Lt. Eric Wilde, conductor and Victor Feldbrill,
violin. Aug. 27, 1943 (PA 152139 Photo by
R.G. Arless)

(PA 174274 photo by R.G. Arless)

Ivan Romanoff of the Navy Show. Aug. 1943
(PA 152135 by R. Arless)

Lt. Oscar Natzke, bass, Nay Show. Ottawa
1943 (Photo by R. Arless)

Producer Lou Silvers of Hollywood with
composer Lt. Quinn. Ottawa 1943 (PA 174273
Photo by R.G. Arless)

Actor Walter Huston with nephew Arthur
Huston. Ottawa 1943 (PA 174270 Photo by
R.G. Arless)

This skit was most impressive to say the least.

To the music of ''Beauty on Duty'' twelve lovely girls
dressed as nurses, walked up the steps facing what appeared to
be a 'reflection' in the huge mirrors on stage. They repeated this
several times and then to the amazement and delight of the
audience, the 'reflections' turned out to be a similar group of
twelve girls moving up and down steps on the other side of the
'mirror' which turned out to be thin gauze curtains throughout
which the other side passed through and joined the other girls in
a closing routine.

BANDS OF THE ROYAL CANADIAN NAVY

List of Second World War bands extracted from book The Naden Band, by CPO2 Jack Mirtle CD LRAM LTCL, published 1990. (With kind permission) HMCS STADCONA: CORNWALLIS: ST HYACINTHE: AVALON: RCN SCHOOL OF MUSIC, TORONTO: PROTECTOR: CHATHAM: SHELBURNE: YORK: NABOB (15 sailors who also manned the guns) BRUNSWICKER (pipe band): NIOBE (stationed overseas at Greenoch, Scotland) PEREGRIVE: ONTARIO (15 sailors afloat who also manned the guns) Alfred E. Zeally made this offer to the Royal Canadian Navy on Oct. 13, 1939. (For complete details see The Naden Band by Jack Mirtle published in 1990. CFB Esquimalt.PMO Victoria. BC VOS LBO) Thanks also to Fred Ashton, Toronto.

H.M.C.S. STADACONA Director Ltd. Commander Alfred E. Zeally. Picture from Norman Fraser (Sarnia). Fraser is trombone player right of flagpole. Band formed in Halifax Jan 8, 1940.

HMCS NADEN On the steps of the Provincial Legislature Building Victoria, B.C. 1st December 1943 Lt (SB) H. Cuthbert. Bandmaster centre-front. (Photo by C.E. Beddoe. Nat. Archives PA 134312) Thanks to Fred Ashton, Toronto.

H.M.C.S. ST. HYACINTHE under training. September 1944 Quebec. (Credit DND Archives PA 131494. Thanks to Fred Ashton, Toronto) ▼

▲ H.M.C.S. CHIPPAWA 1943 Bandmaster Holroyd. Winnipeg, Man. Picture from Norm Foster, Sarnia, Ont.

THE ROYAL CANADIAN AIRFORCE

The Modernaires Dance Band

The Modernaires ranked as a first class dance band even beyond the scope of the R.C.A.F.

The itineraries and duties listed in the Document section outlines their day-to-day activities.

"Took some time digging in places where I haven't looked for years but I found this itinerary and scripts. they aren't in such hot shape...they have yellowed and greyed in the past 45 years." Bob McMullin, Leader. St. Francois Xavier, Man.

The Modernaires, Brussels, Belgium, 1945. ("Ace" Howard)

Trombones. (L to R) Eddie Dunsford, Pete Watt, Ray Miles
Saxes. (L to R) Howard Molstad, Fred Montie, Moe Romanoff, Jim Twitchell
Leader Clarinet Bob McMullin
Trumpets (L to R) Les Allison, Tony Gage, Eugene Cares
Drums Acey Howard
Piano Al Allbut
Guitar Jim Mlodzyk
Bob McMullin died 1989

Members of the "ALL CLEAR" RCAF concert party overseas at Cadogan Gardens, London, England. 1944
Back row A. Weisberd, J. Silverstein, J. Finkleman, Cpl. F. Weaver, LAC J. Kay, LAC B. Bray, LAC R. Lowdon, LAC B McGeary, LAW M. Stephenson, Sgt J. Bickle, LAW B. Parks, LAC V. Zuchter, F/L.A.L. Farenhotz, LAW E. Trundell (husband of) LAC P. Trundell and F/O D. Francis. ▼

Dance Band

THE STREAMLINERS

No doubt one of the finest dance bands of World War II overseas and an example of what a few years experience and togetherness could do for a Canadian group of excellent musicians. It more than equalled the bands of any other country including the U.S.A. and played in the same category as Artie Shaw's Navy Band of that time under the direction of Sam Donahue.

The pictures show the Streamliners playing in Club 21 in Brussels, a Canadian service hostel for troops on leave. In the picture where the band is standing up, a smiling airman can be seen on right centre, with his hands clasped in front of him. This is Bob Burns, a well known Canadian tenor sax player who later played wit the famous Ted Heath band in London as did bassist Jack Fallon also in picture.

"I started at TTS St. Thomas in the brass band and then played string bass in the dance band which became The Streamliners. I remained in England after the war where I played..with Ted Heath, Duke Ellington, etc. and many other top line entertainers..."

Jack Fallon, London, England
Don Hilton, Port Hope.
Thanks also to Paul Grosney
Johnny Bell, Oakville
Len Coppold, New York

The Streamliners, RCAF Playing at Club 21 Brussels. Tour of 1944-45. Pictures from Len Coppold and Lyle Kohler.

Front row: George Lane (Singer), Charlie Overall, Bill Bebington, Mel Smith (Trombones), Phil Sparling, Pat Riccio, Jack Purdue, Frank Palen (Saxes), Lyle Kohler (piano)
Second Row: Frazer Lobban, Bill Carter, Claude Lambert (Trumpets), Don Hilton (Drums), Jack Fallon (Bass), Len Coppold (Guitar)

The W. Debs R.C.A.F. Concert Party

Hazel MacDonald West Vancouver, B.C.

"I was a member of the "W. Debs", a small group at Rockliffe (Canada) in 1943. We were 11 girls and two male pianists. The programme was a variety of skits, songs and dances with violin, piano and accordion. The show went overseas in 1944. It was designed to travel in one bus and one truck for props, etc. We could perform anywhere and we did. An all male group travelled with us at the same time. They were "The Tarmacs"

The girls, Ceci Smith, Audrey Canty and Lennie Barlow tease a Canadian D.R. they called "Dimples".

Photo from Audrey Zilliacus and Eddie Hall.
Audrey Zilliacus (Canty) Ottawa, second from right helps one of the W. Debs put on makeup.

Cpl. Audrey Canty (Ottawa) of the W. Debs, singing at the Stage Door Canteen. Accompanied by RCAF Cpl. Neil Chotem and Sgt Ken Bray (PL 32859 DND) (See also Stage Door Canteen)

Cpl. Audrey Canty (later Sergeant) featured with the W. Debs, Canada, United Kingdom and Europe 1944-45.

"What memories singing and recording so many of those wonderful songs with such accomplished musicians as Neil Chotem, Ken Bray and especially on "Johnny Canucks' Review" (BBC) with Bob Farnon. Being there with such entertainers as Ted (Edmund) Hockridge, Bea Lilie and so many more was the highlight of my entertainment life, not forgetting "W. Debs" where every show we performed is unforgettable for me. We did our very best."

Audrey Zilliacus (Canty) Ottawa

The Tarmacs

HOWARD KARP, MONTREAL

"I sang my way through the war.

I was a Canadian living in Cleveland, Ohio when war broke out and I came to Toronto in September 1939, to join as a fighter pilot. Everybody wanted to be a hero. During training in Trenton, we put on an all male version of "The Desert Song" in which I sang the leading role.

Going overseas in June 1940, most of my singing was done in the pubs, but my big break came one night, August 26th, 1940 (the height of the Battle of britain) while we watched a show in the London Hippodrome during a real massive air raid. We were all told to remain seated and take our chances there rather than go out into the extensive bombing and Vic Oliver (Winston Churchill's son-in-law) who was M.C. asked if anyone wanted to come from the audience. Those airmen who knew of my singing shouted for me to take the stage and I sang "The Donkey's Serenade", then "Begin the Beguine" "When Irish Eyes Are Smiling" and a few others, all the time we were shaking in fear of the bombardment.

The London newspapers wrote about it the next day and the Evening Standard said..".the discovery of a 23 year old member of the Royal Canadian Air Force, Howard Kapinsky, was the sensation of the evening, thanks to Hitler, the war and a Nazi air raid..."

Later I won an amateur contest at the Hammersmith Palais (London), then sang on the bbc and also on a programme with young Vera Lynn. My brother in Chicago just about died when he heard it over the radio.

In May, 1942, I was shipped to remote Ceylon and then in 1943 to Bombay and eventually the same year, back to England where I was assigned to the R.C.A.F. Concert party, "THE TARMACS".

I returned to Canada in January, 1945.

For an entertainer, soldiers are the greatest audiences...We gave them something to laugh at and that made them feel great." Howard Karp.

*From December 12, 1943 to December 30 1944, the Tarmacs gave 274 performances in 375 days to a total of 115,685 troops overseas.

Mickey Mincoff (Dancer), Al Swayze (Regina, Piano), Howard Kapinsky (Karp), Ted Cohen (mike, Winnipeg, M.C.), Lorne Wickie (Montreal, Female Impersonator), George Proulx (Ottawa, drums), Elmer Leadbetter (Sydney, N.S., Cowboy songs, etc.)

Lorne Wickie (Montreal) as female entertainer, Carman Miranda.

▲ Tarmacs, Doing a show and tossing out cigarettes to patients at the No. 8 General Hospital, Bayoux France. Sept. 1944. Pictures Howard Karp.

Master of Ceremonies and comedian of the RCAF all male show The Tarmacs, AC1, Ted Cohen of Winnipeg does a W.C. Fields impersonation (PL 42190 DND).

Patients at 8 General Hospital, Bayoux, France, Sept. 1944. ▼

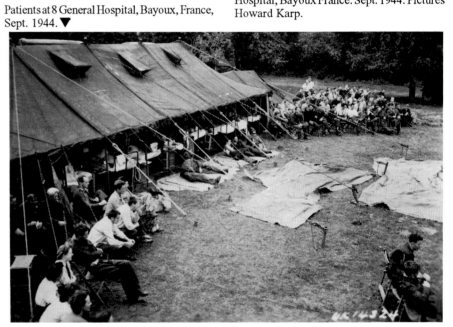

R.C.A.F. Concert Party "The Blackouts"

Photo Sam Levine

Sam Levine, Toronto.

"...I eventually went to The Blackouts..with others such as Hyman Goodman, etc..who were with the ALL CLEAR concert group.

It was an important part of my life although it was entertainment but after all, I was a professional musician at the time.

At first, they felt that the bands were enough but soon realized, like THE ARMY SHOW, that the Air Force also had to have its own groups for travelling..We had some 30 or so people which could be split into two smaller groups as required...

We played for the American Air Force, the R.A.F., as well as our own Canadian units...I remember when Major Bowes (Amateur Radio Hour. New York) auditioned some of us for his show..Ellis McClintok on trumpet, walked away with top honours.

Then we spent 6 months overseas in Europe before returning to Canada some time after the war ended."

R.C.A.F. presents

"Blackouts of 1943"

A MUSICAL REVIEW

Designed for the Entertainment of Air Force Personnel

Under the distinguished patronage of the Governor-General of Canada, His Excellency the Earl of Athlone, K.C., P.C., G.C.B., G.M-M.G., G.C.V.O., D.S.O.

By permission of the Chief of the Air Staff

- PRODUCTION SUPERVISOR
  Squadron Leader N. M. Gilchrist

- DIRECTOR
  Flight Lieutenant R. C. R. Coote

- VOCAL DIRECTOR AND MANAGER
  Flying Officer W. N. M. Campbell

- DANCE DIRECTOR
  Section Officer M. L. A. Thompson

- MUSICAL DIRECTOR
  AC1 G. Calangis

- STAGE MANAGER
  AC2 T. Dowding

- MUSIC ARRANGED BY
  Cpl. K. Bray and Cpl. M. Hyman

- SCENERY DESIGNED BY
  Flight Lieutenant B. Fryer

- COSTUMES AND PROPERTIES
  F.L. Coote, F.L. Fryer,
  S. O. Thompson, Cpl. Dowie

- MUSIC BY
  F.O. Campbell, AC2 H. Singer,
  AC2 S. Levine, LAC R. Horner,
  AC2 J. Gallant

- LYRICS BY
  F.L. Coote, F.L. Fryer,
  F.O. Campbell, AC2 H. Singer,
  AC2 S. Levine, AC2 J. Gallant,
  LAC R. Horner

From Sam Levine

A R.C.A.F. SHOW FOR AIR FORCE PERSONNEL

F.O. WISHART CAMPBELL   S.O. M. L. A. THOMPSON

Sgt. FRAN DOWIE	Cpl. HONOR BENSON	L.A.C. JERRY SHEA
Cpl. HENRY SINGER	L.A.W. MONA MORROW	L.A.C. JOE CARFAGNINI
Cpl. GEORGE CALANGIS	L.A.W. MAXWELL TAYLOR	L.A.C. IRVINE McDOUGALL
Cpl. TERRY DOWDING	L.A.W. EDNA BOND	L.A.C. DANNY McDOUGALL
Cpl. JOHN DOMARACKI	L.A.W. GLORIA HAIGHT	L.A.C. OSCAR BURNSIDE
L.A.C. RONNIE GRAY	L.A.W. FLORENCE SHAW	L.A.C. JACK SAUL
L.A.C. HOWARD JEROME	L.A.W. CECILIA RENNY	L.A.C. ALEX GORDON
L.A.C. SAMMY LEVINE	L.A.W. GEORGETTE GELINAS	L.A.C. STANLEY SOLOMON
L.A.C. MICKEY HORNER	L.A.W. LAVINIA SAWDON	L.A.C. JOHNNY GALLANT
L.A.C. GORDON MOQUIN	L.A.C. GEOFF DAVIS	L.A.C. MITCHELL WEGRZYNOWICZ

◀ From Sam Levine
▼

MADELEINE THEATRE
19, RUE DE SURÈNE, PARIS

★

THE
ROYAL CANADIAN AIR-FORCE
presents
A MUSICAL REVUE

BLACKOUTS

★

PRODUCED AND DIRECTED BY THE
MUSIC AND ENTERTAINMENT BRANCH
OF THE R.C.A.F.

PRESENTED BY THE COURTESY
OF AIR MARSHAL G. O. JOHNSON
A.O.C. IN C R.C.A.F. OVERSEAS
AND R.A.F. 2ND T.A.F. B.L.A.

★

Concert Bands

In 1940, the large Central Band of the RCAF was established in Ottawa under the leadership of Fl/Lt E.A. Kirkwood, the other bands such as the Tactical Air Command Band under Fl/Lt Carl Friberg served in Gander and Edmonton.

The first RCAF band to go overseas was the Overseas Headquarters Band under Sqn. Leader Martin Boundy and went abroad in 1942 followed shortly by the #6 Bomber Group Band under W.O. Clifford Hunt.

The Bournmouth Band under Fl/Sgt S. Voden arrived in 1943.

#6 RCAF Bomber Command W.O.C.O. Hunt. Parading in Yorkshire, England (Photo from Lt/Col. C.O. Hunt)

Massed bands of the Royal Canadian Air Force at Lincoln's Field, England conducted by Sqn Leader Martin Boundy (Photo Lt/Col C.O. Hunt)

Fingal's Follies

D.W. Steeles

''I am a pharmacist now but during the war I trained as air crew in Canada. There were about 250 of us (L.A.C.'s) potential Navigators, Bomadiers, etc. all fresh out of O.T.C. (Officers' Training Club) in Normal School in Toronto, where Ryerson had given us use of their buildings. Then we found ourselves in Fingal (Ont.) for training and all sleeping in a hangar.

About 20 of us organized a stage escapade and our leader was a Mr. Whitehead. We were a chorus line of 'beautiful young males' dressed up as females with short skirts, high heels, etc.

The show was called Fingal's Follies and at first we played for a small group of executive officers along with some people from nearby St. Thomas (Ont.). We were invited to perform in the local theatre and we took up a silver collection for the Red Cross.

The day after the show we were all shipped to Rivers, Manitoba, so maybe we weren't so successful after all but that little splash on the stage was a big relief from the monotony of the camp.
D.W. Steels (Alliston, Ont.)

Sgt Serjent's Trenton

''Music at Trenton (Ont.) was many things. Like the Saracens and crusaders of centuries ago we too had our bands, brass, trumpet and bagpipe. But Music at Trenton was more than that..more than marching and parade square music..It was music in almost every known form. Soothing and stirring classics emanating from 'music appreciation hours' held in the station library, happy sounds of harmonicas, guitars, and accordions played by airmen for their barrack room mates..the sweet song of a W.D. (Womens' Division) entertaining at a station concert..the strident smooth big band sound bursting through the confines of the Sports Hanger as men and women danced to the rhythmic beat..the full throated sound of voices lifted reverently in song at church parades..the raucous shouting and singing in the wet canteens.

It was this and more.''

(Sgt Sergent's Trenton published in 1985 by Hanger Bookshelf 21 Redwing Place, Don Mills, Ont. M3C 2A7)

"Just got your book (Memories and Melodies of World War II) and saw a lot of guys I used to hang out with.

I have attached a list of names of quite a number of the old gang from the RCAF bands and sorry if I have made so much more work for you..it will keep you out of the poolrooms."
Paul Grosney, Willowdale, Ont.

"I was the tenor in two RCAF shows. "Blackouts" and "Out of the Blue""...
Roger Sinclair, McGregor, Ont.

"I served in the RCAF from 1943 to June 1946 and sang with various groups and choirs on each station. In late 1945, I sang with a band in Newfoundland, and we called ourselves the "Navy-Air Force Combo"..apart from playing for our own RCAF messes, etc. we also played for the American units stationed there and the USO in St. John's...Ben Leadbetter was one I remember. He played saxophone and was also the station barber..I have a kitbag of memories, etc. in my basement but I hesitate to go through it..In February, 1945 I was stationed in Sydney N.S. and spent 9 months in hospital after an explosion..Many were killed.."
Brian Edwards, St. Johns, Newfoundland

The RCAF "Swingtime" all male show in England, May,, 1945 at Lincoln's Inn Fields, London; Sgt A.K. Davy (Hamilton), LAC L.G. Killeen (Winnipeg); Cpt F.A. Bestall (Calgary); and W.D. Cpl Margaret Crozier (Toronto) (PL 44252 DND)

Mac Norris

Gay 90's skit by members of "The RCAF Repat Revue at the 126 Wing RCAF Germany Dec. 1945. LAC Kit Murray (Vancouver); LAC Tommy McGee (Toronto); LAC Sheldon Allman (Vancouver); LAW Florence Allen (Toronto); LAC Harvey Perkins (Toronto) ((PL 46471 DND)

Myself and unknown girl singer

Group formed from the RCAF Bomber Command in England.
LAC Charles Woodford, cello, a former member of the BBC Variety Orchestra; LAC Art Sorge (Toronto) with his home made guitar; F/O Harry Lewis (Sault Ste. Marie) piano; and LAC George French, who played with the birmingham Symphony, on violin. (PL 40688 DND)

Gloria Brent, one of Britain's top pop singers with the new "RCAF Show" on the A.E.F.P. radio Network, London, England. LAC Don Alberny of the RCAF Headquarters Band plays piano accompaniment. (PL 33902 DND)

63

Stage Door Canteen

It should also be noted that other Canadian units performed at the American Stage Door Canteen in London, England. The dance bands of the RCAF plus several appearances by the dance band of the Royal Canadian Artillery while stationed in London on the Allied Expeditionary Radio Network.

Canadian born Bea Lillie sitting between Cpl. Audrey Canty and F/O Lola Davis (PL 32865 DND)

E.N.S.A.

The Entertainment National Services Association

Comprised chiefly of World War I leftovers and based on the Victorian and Edwardian era of music halls.

To the newly arriving Canadians in 1939 and 1940, whose only association with entertainment had been the local Bijou on Saturday night watching Dick Powell and the Gold Diggers of 1933 or listening to Bert Pearl and The Happy Gang over the C.B.C. radio, ENSA was a new way of life and a raw experience of sexual frankness akin to prostitution of the arts.

Also, considering the various accents and dialects, much of the show went astray in the translation and interpretation.

General 'Andy' McNaughton made mention at that time that 'he was not satisfied with the type of show ENSA was giving and from his own experience had found them to be extremely rude and vulgar.

This brought about the beginning of Canadian entertainment overseas and the fortunate ending of ENSA within the Canadian services.

The four members of "Rise and Shine" inside caravan which they lived and travelled on the Italian front.
Leslie Dare, Nancy Gisborne, George Maine and Jean Morval. Ortona front. Feb. 3, 1944.
(PA 152156 Photo by D.E. Dolan)

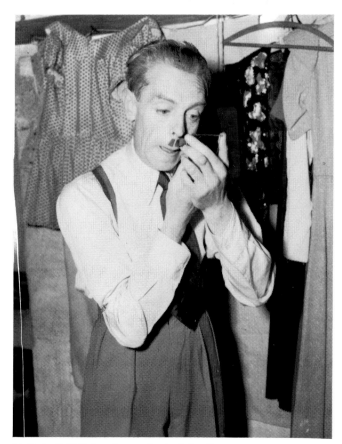

British E.N.S.A. show attached to the Canadian Corp. in Italy. Comedian George Maine dons moustache. Ortona front. Feb. 3, 1944. This unit was named "Rise and Shine"
(PA 152155 Photo by D.E. Dolan)

65

PRISONER OF WAR BANDS

Steve Michell, Huntsville, Ont.

Steve has written an interesting book of his time spent as a German prisoner of war.

The book is titled "They were Invincible" and it is self published at R.R. #4, Huntsville, Ont. P0A 1K0

He was taken prisoner after the tragic attack on Dieppe, Aug. 1942 by the 2nd Canadian Infantry Division. Wounded,, he spent some time in a German hospital and then sent to Stalag 9c where he came across a British bandmaster captured two years earlier at Dunkirk and had formed a band named Britannique. Michell played trombone in one of the army bands and was accepted into the band in Stalag 9c, however he had to obtain special permission from the camp commandant to have his feet and hands untied after the Dieppe raid. The Germans called the Canadians 'bandits' and many were tied for a long period. Many of Michell's tales are humourous as well as grim. Where the Germans made room checks for escape tunnels and ordered everyone out of the room except the band, who unbeknown to the Germans, were sitting on top of an escape hatch playing 'Blue Danube' a favourite of the German guards.

Another time, Michell was about to be transferred to another camp when the commandant said "Nein! Trombone stay!"

The book is well worth reading for a different aspect of a POW.

Bill Cassidy, Maberly, Ont.

"I was a member of the Essex Scottish Regiment from Windsor, Ont. and a friend of mine,, Tony Strauss used to play guitar and piano or accordion in the pubs in England. We did quite a bit of playing in our spare time around Brighton in 1941 and our favourites were "Fools Rush In" "White Cliffs of Dover" and the like.

I was taken prisoner in 1942 on the Dieppe raid and when I was in one of their camps, I bought an old guitar from one of the German guards for some cigarettes. Then the Red Cross supplied us with real good instruments. Padre Foote got a top rated trumpet for our band.

We did different concerts nightly in Stalag VIII B and later moved to Stalag 11D and eventually to Camp 357 in the Polish Corridor near the prot of Danzig. When we went to that camp, 'Lefty' Potts became our leader. He was also from the Essex Scottish band"
Bill Cassidy

THE BEAVER CLUB

The Beaver Club, London, England

"I was a volunteer hostess at the Beaver Club in Trafalgar Square during the war years which was '..a home away from home..' for Canadian servicemen. We put on parties, dances, etc. There was a book called "6 Years and One Day" and I had a copy given to me by Mrs. Vincent Massey, wife of Vincent Massey, then Canada's High Commissioner to Britain.

I marries my husband who was with the Seaforth Highlanders of Canada and so came here was a war bride 45 years ago. You will see a young school girl in one of these pictures sitting on a chair in front of a group of servicemen and women. She came often to the Beaver Club to sing and entertain the Canadians.

She is Petula Clark who has become world famous."

Ruby W. Darvill, Richmond B.C.

CIVILIAN GROUPS

Bluebell Bullets

Organized in Montreal in January, 1941, by members of the staff of Bell Telephone Company, and sponsored by the Bell Auxiliary Aid Association.

For five years they entertained in Canada and performed some 150 shows throughout the country.

On June 24, 1944, a few weeks after "D" Day, they sailed for England and Europe on the "Ile de France" as a civilian concert party attached to the army.

After a number of shows in the Aldershot area in England, they next went to Oldenburgh, Germany, Antwerp, Ghent and other European cities.

Marie Barlow (Lucas),
John Lynham, Willowdale, Ont.
Bell Telephone Historical Service

Manager, Blue Bell Bullets, reports to the President from Germany

OLDENBURGH, Germany,
August 10th, 1945.

Dear Mr. Johnson:

Since last writing to you, we have travelled extensively and seen several interesting countries and put on a few shows. Before leaving the Aldershot area we had a total of fifteen shows to our credit, the greatest number of any concert party.

We arrived at Ostend on July 29th and proceeded to Ghent where we were billeted in No. 2 Canadian General Hospital. Here we were supposed to pick up our generator and a generator operator and move to our starting-off place Thursday. On Tuesday, August 1st, we were informed that we would not leave until Sunday and that our destination would be Oldenburgh, Germany. I asked to be given a show in Antwerp in the meantime, rather than be idle for the week. One of George Grant's workshops is at Antwerp. This show was arranged and we arrived in Antwerp Thursday and found arrangements had been made for a show also on Friday. We put on the two shows, staying overnight, even though we had no clothing or toilet articles with us. Antwerp is badly damaged from V-Bombs, some thirty-five hundred falling in the city.

We returned to Ghent at 2 a.m. Saturday and were advised to be ready to leave by 8.30 a.m. This we did, and travelled across Belgium to the eastern part of Holland where we stayed overnight in a damaged roadside hotel near Lochem. The next morning we proceeded to Germany and arrived at Bad Salzuflen at 6 p.m. We were exceptionally well-quartered here, the army having taken over the best hotels and boarding houses in a very exclusive health resort centre. On the following two nights we put on shows at Lemgo, ten miles distant.

Last Wednesday we arrived at Oldenburgh and performed Thursday night in an old opera house now called Radio City Theatre. We had considerable difficulty in setting up our electrical equipment as the city power is still uncertain and we still lack a generator of our own.

Major-General Vokes was present and came back stage to meet the personnel. He was very pleased with the show. We are rehearsing this afternoon prior to another show tonight.

Tomorrow we go to Aurich for four days, then to Leer for one day and back to Oldenburgh for three more shows, which is the extent of our present schedule. We are the first Canadian civilian concert party to perform in Germany and our reception has been very good. Regardless of the decision not to advertise, we are generally known as *The Blue Bell Bullets* and it is not long before the entire camp knows that we are a Bell Telephone group. Many complimentary remarks are made concerning the company's action in this enterprise.

The health of the personnel is generally good, although one of the male personnel required medical attention this week, which caused him to miss one show.

We were all pleased in a revengeful sort of way to see the great damage done to Osnabruck, although it compared in no way to the destruction of the Rhine cities. At Bad Salzuflen, army personnel carried arms at all times and we were not allowed outside the army compound without armed escort. Here, arms are carried at night and it is considered safe to visit the shops, although there is nothing in them to buy. The people must be living on supplies hoarded in their homes. Cigarettes will secure almost any goods and services, but we are not well supplied as we cannot purchase here on the basis of army personnel.

On the highways large numbers of people of all ages and types are trudging apparently toward their former homes, most of them carrying their possessions on their backs. They are a sullen lot and many whom we have talked to do not feel that they were fairly beaten. Next winter will be one of distress as supplies of all kinds are far below living levels. The field crops, however, in this section look good.

We met a Toronto employee this week and Murray Robertson, former E. A. traffic employee, whom we will again see in Aurich.

I was very sorry to hear of Mr. Collins' illness from George Grant. I will write to him shortly. I will write again in the near future and Mr. Matthews will also be in communication with Mr. Montgomery.

The Bullets Make Good

By E. W. LYMAN

First to cross from Britain to the Continent, first to appear in Belgium where they scored a resounding success at the theatre Cercle Artistique, and first to enter and perform in Germany was the personnel of *The Bullets*, according to first-hand reports reaching Montreal concerning overseas activities of the Canadian civilian army shows.

Letters from performers themselves and unofficial reports coming in regularly tell of enthusiastic welcomes and receptions accorded this overseas unit of the original *Blue Bell Bullets' Revue*, sponsored since 1941 by the Auxiliary Aid Association, Telephone Employees of Montreal Fund. Through recent weeks it has become increasingly apparent that our "Bullets" are doing a bigger and better job than ever the most optimistic of them had dared consider beforehand, and that the enthusiasm of their audiences is greater than they had dreamed possible.

Now swinging into the last weeks of their summertime schedule that opened in Britain early in July and will continue until close to their sailing date on the homeward voyage to land them back in Montreal in early October, *The Bullets* give ample evidence of their delight with the arrangements made for them throughout the European circuit tour. Food and accommodations appear to have greatly exceeded expectations. Transportation has been as convenient and comfortable as conditions would permit. Meantime, they have learned a lot about wartime trouping.

Letters still coming in tell of *The Bullets* having met many former telephone colleagues at many stages in their journeyings. Each has been anxious to know at first hand of the folks back home. For many of these troops overseas a long time, backstage visits with members of the cast and technical staff have been their most satisfying experience in many long months and, in some cases, long years.

Canada Packers

Although not a travelling troupe due to its large scale productions, the Canada Packers Operatic Society did add considerably to the entertainment scene in the Toronto area.

Fully supported by the packing company itself, the operatic society aided in support of the Red Cross, etc.

In one issue of the maple Leaflet, its own newsletter, mention is made of the siege of Leningrad where, despite the 2 year devastation of enemy shelling and air raids, not to mention the freezing winters during which a million died, the two Leningrad symphony orchestras continued to perform on a fairly regular basis proving that the need for music was still a necessity.

James Lynham, Richmond Hill,
Member of the war time cast.

CANADA PACKERS OPERATIC SOCIETY

presents under the direction of

W. R. CURRY

Gilbert and Sullivan's
Celebrated Light Opera

PIRATES of PENZANCE

by permission of Rupert D'Oyly Carte

with excerpts from "Utopia Limited"

EATON AUDITORIUM

College Street

TUES., WED., THURS., FRI., SAT.

FEBRUARY 13 to 17

Evenings - 8:15 p.m.
Matinee - Sat. 2:30 p.m.

ALL SEATS RESERVED
$1.50, $1.00, 75c, 50c (no tax)

NET PROCEEDS FOR CHARITABLE PURPOSES

Chin Up Review

This 1939 show which opened at the Royal Alexander in December had four of the original World War 1 Dumbells in the cast.

Pat Rafferty,, Ross Hamilton, the female impersonator, Red Newman and Jack Ayres.

Roly Young, columnist with the Globe and Mail, Toronto who wrote the column "Rambling With Roly" produced and directed this show where it was held over at the Royal Alex in Toronto for two weeks. It also played as far as Winnipeg and Montreal but due to lack of sponsorship it failed in early 1940.

Kathleen McGregor, Stroud, Ont.

The Eager Beavers

An outstanding civilian concert party formed by members of the Sun Life Assurance of Canada with head offices in Montreal. After many successful performances in Canada, they were advised in February,, 1945 to be prepared for overseas service. Although a civilian organization, they were then attached to the military and had to remove any indication of their sponsors. At the same time other groups such as BLUE BELL BULLETS, (Bell, Telephone), LEGION ALL STARS (Canadian Legion) THE MASQUERS (T. Eaton) LIFEBUOY FOLLIES, (Proctor and Gamble) and THE COMBINES, (Massey Harris) also became part of the military for overseas service.

With the end of the war (May 8, 1945) in sight and, as a result, the veteran bands, soldier concert parties, etc., many of whom had been overseas since 1939, were now being broken up and returned to Canada, a desperate need for entertainment was evident and so the civilian shows were being brought into overseas action. This was a great leap from being an 'amateur' show to suddenly becoming involved in what was professional work.

Under the apt direction of Herbert J. Ward, who wrote and produced the show and also a member of the Sun Life Company himself, The Eager Beavers excelled in their performances with the troops overseas.

FROM MARIE BARLOW (NEE LUCAS) LONDON, ONT.

"In March of 1945 we put on 4 shows in the Sun Life Auditorium to cover expenses of curtains, props, etc.

Smutty jokes or too skimpy costumes were 'frowned' upon. As I wasn't 21 my parents had to sign a release form. We were all issued 2 sets of military uniforms although we were still members of the Sun Life Company and our company salaries were deposited to our bank accounts while we lived as army personnel.

On our way over when the train reached Moncton, an army officer decided we should stretch our legs and took us on a route march. We never had any training for this and the march was horrible. We sailed on the "Ile de France" and did several shows on board as dress rehearsals only and danced on mess tables pushed together with soldiers stationed to catch us if we fell. When we got off the train in Aldershot, England, we were picked up by the MP's (Military Police) and put into an army stockade until later our liaison officer came to collect us.

On July 28th we headed for the Continent with half a dozen 60 cwt trucks and because we were civilians we had to pass through customs!

We were first stationed at the #2 Canadian General Hospital and after three days found that the men had a bathtub in their section. They agreed to switch with us but who was to get the first bath? We had over 100 girls from all concert parties so we drew lots for turns. I drew #54 and my bath time was 3:30 am to 3:45 am. Joy!

We got ticks from old mattresses in Holland and there was always the problem of baths.

We played at Varel, Oldenburg, Wilhellmshaven, Hilversum, Appeldoorn, Nijmegan, Arnhem, Brussels, Amsterdam, Ostende, etc. and returned to England by landing craft LST."

From *Kay Hoskins* (nee Ward) Kingston, Ont.

"I am the girl (in the picture) on the left side with her arm resting on the wall...

I was the youngest at 19 and was allowed to go overseas because my father Herbert (Bert) Ward was the director of the show.

We travelled around the military bases in Canada for 2 years before going overseas."

Thanks also to Norman C. Galey
Archivist. Sun Life Assurance

Some of the Cast shortly after their arrival in England. Left to right: Kay Ward, Daisy Miller, Sheila Galbraith, Margaret Blois, Dorothy Johnston, Marie Lucas, Cathy Fullerton, Gert Thomas, Mae Kelly. In the Right foreground: Ernie Crowe (Business Manager).

PA 152136 Photo by Arthur L. Cole, July, 1945

Soestdijk, Holland, August 13. 1945

FROM KAY WARD

KAY WARD

"The trip across here was wonderful. We came over on the 'Ile de France' and had grand weather every day. No one seasick (honest). You should have seen us at life-boat drill wearing our lifebelts every morning; we looked like Mr. Five-by-Five. We had to be in bed at eleven every night, and they turned off all the water and light at 10.30 p.m. Adele and I found that out the hard way. We were very busily washing in the cabin when suddenly the lights went out, the water was turned off, and there we were with soap in our eyes groping around in the dark.

"We landed at Greenock July 2nd and were immediately put on a train for Aldershot. I spent the week-end in London, saw all the famous places and also all the bombed-out places. I couldn't begin to tell you what it was like. Whole blocks of houses blown to the ground, trees and poles flung by the roadside, wrecked trains. It was grim. At Aldershot we lived in cute little houses, six or seven to a house. I guess Canadian girls were scarce there because Canadian soldiers would come up and say 'Gee, real Canadian girls! Say something. We just want to hear you talk!'

1945 *Aug. 30.*

"Yesterday I arranged a baseball game between an impromptu team of our girls and the Officers of the Regina Rifles. It was played at the Reginas' sports field at Ede and was more fun than a picnic. I have sent an account of it to one of the sub-editors of the 'Maple Leaf' whom we met in Ghent and Brussels. Also a film unit took four or five pictures of the highlights of the game and I miss my bet if one or more does not make the illustrated papers in Canada.

"The game was played for the entertainment and amusement of the 'other ranks' of the Regiment and the girls won 15 to 12, but the officers and umpires were undoubtedly more affected by the players than by the ball. Many of the girls had little knowledge of the game and some of their remarks were priceless. When the umpire said 'Batter up', Kay Ward, on second base, was heard to say 'Well, he might at least say please!' Florence Katsunoff was left stranded on 2nd base when the third 'out' came via the strikeout method. As the officers trotted off the field, she shouted—'Hey, you can't *do* that, I'm still out here!' In the last inning anything went and the girls got a couple of 'outs' by mobbing the base-runner and, by female force, keeping him off the base until the outfielders threw the ball in. One of the pictures illustrated such a play."

From the Diary of a Trooper Edna Wootan.
(Town of Mont Royal.)

On board the S.S. "Ile de France" June 26, 1945

"Have been on our way for two days now...Assembled in Montreal, Sunday afternoon...extremely self conscious in khaki (uniform) with kit bags crammed full..My baggage consists of a haversack and a large suitcase and the dignity of my departure was utterly ruined when I had to be tugged from above and shoved from below to get up the steps with my burden...In Halifax we got marching orders. The pacemaker must have been a racehorse..within seconds all was utter confusion". (The girls were civilians put into uniform only for the purpose of going overseas.)

June 28, 1945
"War in Europe is over....Emergency boat drill..Dorothy was in the shower and decided to go down with the ship...

August 1, 1945
"Big day in my life..I had a bath."
The complete diary of Edna Wooten is worthy of a book on the subject of overseas service for the girl show...Keeping off the hungry soldiers, trying to find regular baths, attacked by 'harvest mites', the two Belgian plumbers who feel free to walk in on a shower room for 'inspection' whenever they wish, a drinking scene in a skit where water was well salted without their knowledge, and so on.

Thanks to Edna Wooten.

SUN LIFE REVUE

Director	BERT WARD
Consulting Director	EDWYN WAYTE
Assistant Director	DAVID MATHESON
Dance Directress	HILDA GALT
Musical Director	TOMMY SIMPSON

OPENING	Singers and Dancers
HE FORGOT	Hugh and Leslie
TRIO	Florence, Thelma, Jean
LAST BULLET	An Affair with the Foreign Legion
FLORADORA	Dancers
SONG	Jean Wood
UNCLE ELMER	Rustic Scene
KISS ME	Marguerite Chaillot
OH DOCTOR!	Dorothy, David, Edna and Hugh
CONGA	Singers and Dancers

(Specialty Dance — DIANA FORBES)

INTERVAL

SEASIDE	Gay Nineties
SONG	Florence
HILL-BILLY	Poetic Interlude
JITTERBUGS	Adele and Marcel
DRAMATIC RECITAL	Selected
BOWERY	Dancers
WINNNIE	David and Leslie
DREAMLAND	Singers
PRECISION	Dancers
CHEERIO	"The Old School Tie"
FINALE	Singers and Dancers

SUN LIFE REVUE

ENTERTAINMENT COMMITTEE

NORMAN GILLESPIE	Chairman
JOAN WARD	Vice-Chairman
ADAM MEIKLEJOHN	Road Manager

Singers

JEAN CLAYTON	DOROTHY JOHNSTON
THELMA DAVIES	FLORENCE KATSUNOFF
JEAN DRUMMOND	JEAN WOOD
MARGARET HABKIRK	CARLETTE SAUERBRUNN

Dancers

EVIE BAMFORD	DAISY MILLER
MARGUERITE CHAILLOT	ADELE PAQUIN
SIMONE DIMITRI	KAY WARD
DIANA FORBES	MARGARET WEBSTER
EILEEN KYLE	BARBARA WOOD
EILEEN MAHONEY	DOROTHY WOODWARD

MARCEL LONGTIN

Comedy

EDNA WOOTAN	DAVID MATHIESON
LESLIE ELVIDGE	HUGH LAYHEW

JOHNNIE CALDWELL — Drums

Backstage

BERT WOODWARD — Stage Manager	DICK BORLAND — Electrician
LESLIE FORTH	HARRBY BROWN	BILLY KERRY

NESSIE WOTHERSPOON — Wardrobe Mistress

LOUIE MEIKLEJOHN	GERT THOMAS

SIMONE LANGEVIN — Properties

Message from Capt. G. H. BOYD, District Administrator

"The complete Staff and Personnel of this Hospital join with me in expressing our sincerest appreciations and thanks to all those who have been responsible for the Sun Life Revue coming to Ste. Anne's, also to those tireless workers who entertain us. Especially so to-night, will those who often are unable to attend the regular performance feel gratified, because to-night we are making the show 'their night'."

Calgary Elks Concert Party

"My father and my husband's father (Art Curtis and Jack Girvin) were both members of the Elks Concert Party which began sometimes in the '30's...Josh Henthorne was the master of ceremonies and also announcer for the Calgary Stampede for many years.."

Pat Girvin, Victoria, B.C.

CHRISTMAS 1941
Dear Art:

At this time I wish to express my hearty appreciation to you for your wonderful cooperation in putting over the various concerts given to entertain His Majesty's Forces. They have brought forth numerous favourable comments from the various officers commanding.

Thanking you and with best wishes for a Merry Christmas and a Happy New Year,

Yours sincerely,

Josh Henthorne

74

The Fragments

Formed by Douglas Park in 1940 in Victoria, B.C. under the auspices of the Britannia Branch of the Canadian Legion. Later changed name to THE VERSATILES. Every Friday night they went to one of the nearby army camps who were being prepared for overseas service. Sometimes when the troops were 'confined to barracks' the concert party would be called upon to do extra shows for the 'restless ' soldiers.

The last concert was given for released prisoners of war from Japan on the ship "Gripsholm".

Front row: Mary Armitage, ? Grace Adams, Bert Lashmar, Dorothy Finn, Muriel Jarvis.
Rear: Les Dash, ?, Alf Adams, Doug Park, Jim Matheson, ?, George Todd.
Mary J. Park, Victoria, B.C.

The Fragments

The Freedomaires

Formed in the '30's as The Baby Capitolians and The Winnipeg Kiddies who performed dance numbers in the Capitol, Metropolitan, Orpheum and Walker theatres.

When war broke out in 1939, their leader and director, Fleurette McCaig (later married as Kramer) had over 100 trained dancing girls complete with their own tights, veil and ballet slippers. They joined the branch of the Canadian Army Special Services to entertain troops and train members of the Womens' Army Corp. (C.W.A.C.). The group toured thousands of miles in Manitoba and Saskatchewan, dancing not only for Canadians but also English, Dutch and other nationalities training in Canada. When the war was over they each received a certificate (as shown) for their wartime entertainment services.

Fleurette McCaig-Kramer, Mississauga, Ont.
Grace Tyre (nee Gjolstad), Winnipeg, Man.

The Lifebuoy Follies

Sponsored by Lever Brothers

Formed in 1941 as one of the efforts of business to become involved with troop entertainment through the use of civilian staff which later found it necessary to don military uniform and proceed overseas to add to the every increasing need of Canadian forces entertainment.

The Lifebuoy Follies spent four years on the road in Canada during which time they performed to over half a million Army, Air Force and Navy personnel throughout Canada and Newfoundland.

They went wherever they could go either by jeep, boat, train and plane. One hundred and fifty Red Cross shows were also presented and the troupe donated every penny of their paid engagements to the Red Cross in the amount of $42,000.00. The Canadian Legion War Services invited the Lifebuoys to entertain overseas and this is one of the programmes.

The show was produced by World War I veteran entertainer, Jack McLaren who was a prime director of the famous Dumbells.

From Daphne Cameron (nee MacFarlane)

"I joined Lifebuoys in 1942 but I was entertaining at the age of 14 so I was very young when I took part in the show...I joined the "Skating Scandals" in Toronto then had a call from Lever Brothers to become part of their show. We went as far as Alaska and east to Newfoundland..

In 1945 we went overseas and I don't think we missed a service camp or unit in all of England or Scotland. It was a time I will never forget. The most rewarding performances were in the military hospitals. I will never forget the ravages of war and the inhumane sufferings (we came across) overseas. Jack Ayres of world War I Dumbells, was our early pianist and also Pat Rafferty, another famous Dumbell who was with us in the initial stages. I have often hoped we could have a reunion and I am working on that. I am terribly sorry that I can find no pictures of the Lifebuoys."

Daphne Cameron, Elmsdale, N.S.

The Masquers

The Masquers was formed and sponsored by the T. Eaton Co. of Montreal and all members of the troupe were also on the staff of T. Eatons.

They entertained from September 12, 1940 to June 6, 1945, and in Canada they travelled some 30,000 miles by bus, train and truck.

It was originally planned for performance at the Y.M.C.A. Service Club on Phillips Square in Montreal and their first skit was called The Red Triangle but so great was the demand for troop entertainment, they soon found themselves constantly on the move across Canada entertaining at the numerous and various military depots. After five years of entertaining in Canada, the Masquers of Eatons, Toronto joined forces with the Montreal group and proceeded overseas in June 1944 where they entertained over 90,000 Canadian servicemen in England, Belgium, Holland and Germany. They did a total of 114 shows before being returned home to Canada.

On April 25, 1945, the 300th performance of The Masquers took place at Vimy Camp in Kingston, Ont. and they gave their last show on June 6, 1945 at the Columbus Hall in Montreal. They then disbanded and returned to their respective jobs with Eatons.

Marjorie Hilton (Nee Gonnett), Peterborough, Ont.

Montreal Masquers and poster. Kay Quinn, Shirley Reilly, Lil Evans, Betty MacDonald, Gwyn Drummend, Olive Mancher, Shirley Gireux, Fleurette Piche. Holland. October 17, 1945 (PA 17433 Photo)

Rhythmcade

"We were a small group of teenagers, students from Eastern Commerce, Malvern Collegiate, Danforth Tech and a few other high schools, who donated their time and talent for this show.

We travelled by Gray Coach bus, driven by Andy Baptie, who was very much liked for his kindness and who always drove every student right to their doors after every performance.

We played and danced in the army and airforce bases in Southern Ontario from 1943 to 1945 including Manning Depot, Camp Borden, Trenton, Picton, Belleville, Deseronto, Newmarket, Brampton, Mount Hope, etc.

We had six dancers with Mr. Craig Hamilton as leader of the chorus. Originally his choir was called THE BEACHES YOUTH CHORUS. Louise Burns was our dance instructor.

We once got stuck in the snow at Camp Borden and had many similar problems in travelling but Louise Burns gave us each a skein of wool to knit long scarves for the soldiers overseas, so we had little time to worry.

We made our own gowns, etc. but later, Mr. Brockie, head of merchandising at T. Eatons, Toronto, arranged for all costumes and gowns to be supplied free.

After 50 shows we were each given a pin "THE CITIZENS COMMITTEE FOR TROOPS IN TRAINING" presented at the Salvation Army by Lady Kemp at Castle Frank on Bloor St."

Doris Carr (Scarborough, Ont.)

Stand Easy

A camp concert party formed by several members of the Armed Forces and civilian staff at Petawawa Camp, Ontario in 1941.

"I was in the Royal Canadian Engineers Band at Petawawa Camp when Peter Greisman, Chris Lovett and Don Sexton put together a good show called "STAND EASY"...I played in the group accompanying the show and we had expected it to go on the road to other camps, etc. We did a few one nighters in the Ottawa Valley area but the group was broken up into smaller units which did travel around...but by that time I had been transferred to the RCAF for flight crew training..."

Ed Terziano, Huntsville, Ontario

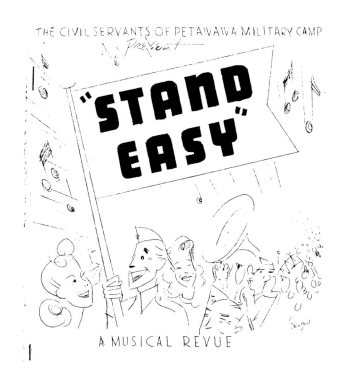

THE CIVIL SERVANTS OF PETAWAWA MILITARY CAMP present

"STAND EASY"

A MUSICAL REVUE

Produced And Directed by L/Bdr. Pete Greisman	
Musical Direction & Scoring by Gnr. Chris Lovett	Stage Scenery & Sets Designed by L/Bdr. Don Sexton
Stage Manager	Lieut. F. Dysart
Dancer	Percy Palevski
Costumes	Mrs. Holt Barlow and Miss Heather Forgie
Tailoring	R.C.O.C. (C.S. Tailoring)
Set Construction	Camp Engineers
Installation of Lights	Mr. F. Pierce

The Civil Servants' Club of Petawawa Military Camp

Present

"Stand Easy"
A Musical Revue in Three Acts
Camp Auditorium

With the kind permission of
Brigadier W.C. Thackray
Commander
Petawawa Military Camp

Tin Hat Review

This Tin Hat Revue is not to be mistaken for The Tin Hats who were a Soldier Concert Party overseas.

Formed in October 1939, they played free weekly shows for the services and by 1943 had performed 165 shows to over 200,000 troops in Canada.

Imperial Tobacco sponsored much of the show such as paying for costumes, sets and sound equipment.

It is interesting to note than a number of these 'civilians' later joined the armed forces as entertainers. Bob Goodier and John Pratt became leading members of the "MEET THE NAVY SHOW" and it was Pratt who performed the show stopping act of "You'll Get Used To It" for which he wrote the text to music by Freddy Grant.

Pratt used it first as a civilian performer with the Tin Hat Revue.

The Victory Entertainers Carry On Review Thumbs Up Review Whiz Bang Review

The four groups came from the Hamilton, Ontario area and were sponsored by the Hamilton Citizens' Committee.

They were formerly disbanded in June of 1946 however many of the personnel carried on by themselves in order to entertain and cheer the many war veterans still in hospitals.

They travelled over 80,000 miles during the war years and brought entertainment to almost 1 million servicemen and women in Canada.

CARRY ON REVIEW
Formerly known as the Merry Madcaps Review, they gave their first performance in early 1941. Proctor and Gamble sponsored this.

THUMBS UP REVIEW
In March on 1940, Doreen Groom and Gordon Anderson, of the Vi Tone Company, organized this show, which continued for six years.

THE VICTORY ENTERTAINERS
Formed at the very beginning of World War II in 1939 and their first show came a few weeks after Canada's entrance into the War (Sept. 10, 1939). They gave their first show on Sept. 28, 1939 in Stanley Barracks, Toronto.

THE WHIZ BANG REVIEW
Organized later in early 1943 and gave its first show at the RCAF camp in Mount Hope. Quite a number of this unit came from the other three and joined when it was realized that more entertainment was required.

The dancers are from the Nancy Campbell Studios of Hamilton.

Veronica Marchildon (nee O'Donnell), Burlington, Ont.

Pictures and programmes from Veronica Marchildon, Burlington, Ont.

Lorrain Lombard, Ruth Shackleton, Ruth Cole, Dorothy Jenkins, Velma Lombrad, Veronica O'Donnell (Marchildon)

CARRY ON REVIEW

VICTORY ENTERTAINERS

Formed in the Montreal High School in the early part of the war, this dance band played for many troop dances including the CPR Club.

Oscar Peterson was on piano and lead trumpet was Maynard Ferguson. Percy, Maynard's older brother led the band. Maynard also used to play the bugle calls for the school during the raising and lowering of the flag even in the bitter cold of winter. Oscar Peterson, would stand inside the glass door and laugh at him.

Don Cameron was drummer with the band at that time.

DON CAMERON, Toronto.

THE VICTORY ENTERTAINERS

Dorothy Jenkins and Veronica O'Donnell (Marchildon)

THE VICTORY ENTERTAINERS

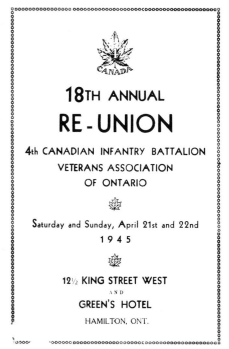
18TH ANNUAL
RE - UNION
4th CANADIAN INFANTRY BATTALION
VETERANS ASSOCIATION
OF ONTARIO

Saturday and Sunday, April 21st and 22nd
1945

12½ KING STREET WEST
AND
GREEN'S HOTEL
HAMILTON, ONT.

79

Victoria Girls' Drill Team

''The Victoria Girls' Drill Team was formed in 1938 so when the war broke out in 1939, we were already prepared. My father died during the war and both of my older brothers never returned home. One was lost at sea and my elder one killed in action at Scapa Flow.''

        MARY BULMER, Victoria, B.C.

VICTORIA DAILY TIMES Tuesday May 9, 1944

'As the dusk began to veil the mountains in the background...a girl's voice sang out 'The Lord's Prayer'. In front of her, silent and touched sat an audience of sun tanned soldiers. When Helen McNaught had finished her song,..a roar of appreciation went up.

    It was a great reward for the 22 girls of the Victoria Girls' Drill Team who had driven up island to entertain the troops...Leaving the highway to come out beneath the Forbidden Plateau, the girls had bounced and jogged along in their bus with two jeeps leading the way and flagging them past the potholes along the logging trail. When the bus could go no farther, soldiers swarmed around and carried the equipment on their shoulders, pushing their way through the forest until they reached a clearing. The girls sang songs until 2:30 in the morning.'

Victoria Girls' Drill Team
Thanks to Mary Bulmer, Victoria, B.C.

MISCELLANEOUS

AUDREY PULLIN
Audrey sang with the band of The Royal Canadian Artillery a number of times over the Allied Expeditionary Radio Network (Canada) during the 1944 time of the London V 1 rockets, the buzz bombs. She also was a very busy soprano with a variety of programmes entertaining the troops.

"Highlight of the programme at the Queensbury Club was the singing of W.R.E.N. Audrey Pullin, which brought thunderous applause from the servicemen audience when she sang "My Hero" from The Chocolate Soldier. That this twenty two year old singer should steal a show from a line up of very popular troopes, was amazing.

Audrey voluntarily sings on her own time without special leave to camp concerts and troops everywhere."
DICK GORDON. Stage, Screen and Studio, 1944

EUNICE DAVIES
This vivacious 18 year old redhead entertained the troops in and around Toronto, particularly at Christie Hospital where so many wounded Canadians were stationed.

With a sweet lyric Welsh soprano and accompanied by piano, she was the Jeanette MacDonald of Dewi Sant (St. David) as she sand such familiar songs as "Kiss Me Again" "Sweetheart" "My Hero" and other such melodious songs of that time.

In 1948 she married the author and changed her name to Stephens.

LIA DORANA

During the time the Royal Canadian Artillery dance band played in the officers's hotel, the Grande Gooiland in Hilversum Holland, the officer in charge of entertainment Capt. Thompson decided to add a female singer to the Canadian band. This was Dutch vocalist Lia Dorana. See story in author's Harps of War. Lia is still starring in major roles in Europe.

ANNA MOSER (Oakville)

Wartime entertainment does not belong to one side only, as in the case of ANNA MOSER **, our next door neighbour who came from Germany after World War II, with husband John.

Both had been taken prisoners of war in December 1944 while working on a Danube shipyard caught in between the advancing Russians and the German defenders. Anna was just 16 years old.

After many camps, they ended up in #1551 in Harko in the Ukraine where a musician named Ukrk formed a small orchestra.

"I played drums!" Anna announced proudly "They were made out of big steel shells and what a boom it made!"

In the group was one priest, Father Halter, who later came to Canada and died in 1989 in Windsor, Ontario. He played a hand made violin while another priest played guitar. The most popular piece of music was "Roll Out The Barrel" which of course is an original German composition.

John and Anna were released in November 1949, four years after the war after serving 5 years of slave labour. They married and came to Canada. Note a good picture but a most historical one. Note banner of Stalin in background. (** author)

BONNIE WARD TROUPE

"I was only 9 when the war broke out but I did do volunteer shows from 1941 to 1945. I was studying ballet and acrobatics at the Wynne Show Studios in Victoria (BC) (I did go on to teach there from the age of 16 to 21)

I remember doing acrobatic solos, tap dancing and solo Can Can. We had BONNIE WARD, DOROTHY DAVIES (comedienne) FRED USHER and his Western Music group, and many others."

DOREEN KEATING (Bull) (Victoria, B.C.)

THE MUSIC OF WORLD WAR II

While we remember the most nostalgic of songs from that period, such as "Quartermaster Stores" "Lilli Marlene" "Nightingale Sang In Berkeley Square" "White Cliffs of Dover" and many others, there were probably thousands of songs written and now forgotten.

One of the oddities of showbusiness, either in war or otherwise, is that every musician feels he is capable of writing the 'big hit' and so in the many hundreds of concert parties, shows, etc. not only in Canadian ones but universally, the songwriter and the lyricist plugged away continuously striving for that elusive goal of fame and fortune.

That is not to say, their works were not without worth. Of course, many and most were without worth but nevertheless there were good songs and even great songs. The problem was exposure. Irving Berlin had great songs but he also had great exposure. Other songs became famous and well known usually through the movies or radio.

Even as far back as the American Civil War when Walter Kittridge wrote "Tenting In the Old Campground" it was exposure. He paid the singing Hutchinson Family the sum of $500.00 to promote wherever they went and since they were the Number 1 on the Civil War hit parade, the song became famous.

Unfortunately, Canadians had no such exposure. When the war ended so did their dreams of future 'world' appreciation as songwriters. One big Canadian song did make it. "I'll Never Smile Again" by Toronto's Ruth Lowe but only because Frank Sinatra recorded it with Tommy Dorsey.

A PATRIOTIC SONG
"My father 'PERCY BENNETT', played in a Canadian Arm Band in World War I and continued to be interested in music during World War II. He was teacher of maths at the WD Lowe Technical School in Windsor, Ont. and was also in charge of assembly music.

He composed one song A PATRIOTIC SONG in 1941 and then, when a cousin enlisted in the RAF he wrote "MEN OF THE RAF" for the Doncaster (Yorks) segment. It became the official song and included many Canadians integrated into the RAF."
(PATRIOTIC SONG MEN OF THE RAF)
MARGARET A. BENNETT (Ottawa)

"I enclose a copy of a war song written and dedicated to the honour of the 57th and 59th Heavy Artillery Regiments of Newfoundland in 1942. Worlds by W. Barker and music by Bdr (Corporal) J. Barter. It was written in 1940 prior to our (Newfoundland) joining Canada in 1949"
MARCHING TOGETHER
WILLIAM E. PARSON, Harbour Grace (Nfld)

(*For further reference on World War II songs see author's book MEMORIES AND MELODIES OF WORLD WAR II published by Boston Mills Press. 1987)

MARCHING TO-GETHER
A Song

Words by W.H. BARTER

PRICE 50 CENTS

Music by BDR. J. BARTER

CANADA'S FORGOTTEN WOMEN
Lois Laycock, Richmond, Ont.

Lest we forget!
The women of this land
Who in Canada's time of need.
Extended a helping hand

The WACS, WAFS, the WRENS,
Special ladies were they all
Undaunted by the winds of war
Answered their country's call.

How priceless were these women
They took the avid stand
And forged ahead with courage
To serve a country grand.

While here at home
Far away from war and strife
Women worked from dawn to dusk
With visions of a brighter life.

Salute to the mothers
who kept the homes with pride
Dried our tears and calmed our fears
And strengthened family ties.

Lest we forget, the volunteers
That packed with special care
Things to wear, things to read
For our loved ones over there.

Be proud, women of Canada
Sisters, wives and mothers
March with your flags held high
With soldiers, vets and others.

Used with kind permission.

WARTIME MEMORIES   Lois Laycock, Richmond, Ont.

In memory, I travel back in history
The years are many, the miles are long
Men fought for King and Country
To make it great and ever strong.

The Air Force were courageous men
Flying Aces in the sky
Forming paths of silver winds
Like eagles on a mountain high.

The Gray fog casts a mystic spell
White gulls circle wide and free
The Navy escorted the convoys
Through the squalling winds of the sea.

Some men chose the soldier's life
Upon a strange and foreign land
Where blood marked the lonely trail
Worn deep across the sand

Past memories, many years
The tireless battle through the winter snows.
Deepen the tracks where soldiers trod
Pursued its course and onward goes.

Hold still the dawn!
A soldier was heard to cry
the wind went sighing overland
As they laid him down to die.

No homecoming for this comrade
No poppies adorn his grave
But with a sombre, heavy heart
A sad goodbye to a soldier brave.

Silently, the guns ceased firing
As war time shadows were giving way
To a world filled with endless hope
That peace was here to stay.

We are the heirs of a free nation
Men struggled, fought and died
For us to live in security
With loved ones by our side.

Used with kind permission

84

World War II tank, the Holy Roller, as it now sits in retirement in Victoria Park, London, Ontario. Several bullet marks are visible up front. (Picture by W. Ray Stephens)

THE HOLY ROLLER

In Victoria Park, London, Ontario, sits a World War II tank called "The Holy Roller". Apart from the battlescars of Europe, the Holy Roller also has a small portion of musical interest as well.
From HERB MAQUIRE, London, Ont.

"I joined the 1st Hussars Tank unit in London and also played in the band for a while until we went overseas in 1941 where we managed to scrape up our own dance orchestra of eight members. LOU GRAYLING was leader, with GROD TRICKER and BUD HATHAWAY on trumpets, MEL HAINES on drums, BOBBY REARDON piano, BUS FOWLER guitar, myself on bass and fiddle with SAM PAWLEY on vocals.

Both Bud and Bobby were Americans and went over to the U.S.A. Forces in England when they came over.

Without the band, Bus Fowler and myself, played around the pubs in England for free drinks and fun.

Bus drive the tank "The Holy Roller" now sitting in Victoria Park here, while I drove a scout car. We carried our fiddle and guitar with us and in between battles we got together to entertain some of our own troops as we rested up for the next onslaught.

"The Holy Roller" was brought back from the war in Europe and put in Victoria Park."

Herb MacQuire (London, Ont.)

THE QUEENSBERRY CLUB.
LONDON, ENGLAND

The home of the rules of boxing became an entertainment club between 1942 and 1945.

MR. WINSTON CHURCHILL
"The very large number of men and women of the Allied Fighting forces who have been entertained...shows on how broad a scale this work has been carried out..."

GENERAL EISENHOWER
"On behalf of the United States Forces, European Theatre, I should like to express the gratitude...of the unlimited ..entertainment.."

MR. A.V. ALEXANDER First Lord of the Admiralty
"In the heart of London..a centre to which thousands of serving men have turned to get relief..from war.."

Massed drum and bugle band of the 3rd Canadian Division passing Buckingham Palace, London, Ont. October 23, 1941 (PA 145335 Photo By O.C. Hutton)

NO 1 CANADIAN ARTILLERY HOLDING UNIT
Concert party under Lou (Pops) Hooper.
Gave a performance in the Cambridge Theatre
in London
Louis Stanley Hooper.

French Canadians in Forestry Corps Orchestra. Ecosse. June 1943
(PA 152166 Photo by T.F. Rowe)

Five civilian concert groups. Adele Paquin (Eager Beavers), Rolande Lavergne (Bluebell Bullets), Shirley Anderson (Masquers), Irene Hughes (Follies), Ramona Hodges (Combines); Aldershot, England July 4, 1945 (PA 152134 Photo by Arthur Cole)

German Tiger tank and grave of one of the tank's crew. Italy 1944. Taken by Terrence Spencer of Bandoliers Concert Party.

Hungry European children foraging in left over mess tins for food. (W.R. Stephens)

The Grand Hotel Gooiland in Hilversum, Holland where the Royal Canadian Artillery dance band began playing for officers' dances, a few days after Liberation. It contained a spacious dining room where only bread and bully beef was served and a small group played there. An English woman on piano who had been there all through the war, a romantic Italian violinist and a young Javanese zimabalist.

The dance band played in an adjoining room leading out to a large movie theatre and also a big concert hall.

The programme attached was presented through the sponsorship of the Canadian Army on May 20th, 1945, two weeks after V.E. Day. Note in picture postcard, the proprietor can be seen standing on far right smoking a cigar. Apparently it meant little to him if there were Germans or Canadians in his hotel.

Even the enemy made music. German prisoner playing guitar en route to Canada. Feb. 7, 1945 (PA 152126 photo by A.M. Dare)

Hilversum, Holland had been the radio centre before the war and there were quite a number of pre-war musicians in the area such as an elderly gentleman string bass player who had worked on the railroad all through the war.

The Canadian Army organized the symphony within days after Liberation. They gave their first performance as per programme just two weeks later. The author took along a happy young group of his Dutch family Verbeek.

The concert was held in the splendid theatre of the Grand Hotel Gooiland. AT the same time, another division of the Canadian Army had assembled a disbanded midway and fair in Hilversum and again, the Canadians and their adopted Dutch families, particularly the young, found out what 'liberation' really meant.

ON SUNDAY THE 20th OF MAY
will play for you

HUGO DE GROOT
AND HIS SYMPHONY ORCHESTRA
at 2000 Hours in Grand Theatre Gooiland

Programme

1. Overture to the opera „Zampa"   Louis Hérold
2. Intermezzo from the opera „Cavalleria Rusticana"
                                          Pietro Mascagni
3. Air of Figaro from the opera „The Barbier of Seville"
   (by the Bariton Henk Dorel)   G. Rossini
4. Tales from the Vienna Woods, Waltz   Johann Strauss
5. Irish Tune from County Derry, arranged by Percy Grainger
   (for String Orchestra)
6. Land of Hope and Glory – March –   Edward Elgar

———

1. Nutcracker Suite, from the Ballet „Casse Noisette"
                                          Peter Tchaikovsky
   I   Miniature Overture
   II. Characteristic Dances
        a. March
        b. Dance of the Sugar plum fairy
        c. Russian Dance (Trepak)
        d. Arabian Dance
        e. Chinese Dance
        f. Dance of the „Mirletons"
   III. Flowerwaltz   (By special request)
2. Negro Lullaby   Clutsam
   (by the bariton Henk Dorel)
3. Overture from the Operette „Orpheus in the Underworld"
                                          Jaques Offenbach
4 Hands across the Sea – March –   John Philip Sousa

14th Bty, Rainbow Review of the 5th Anti/Tank Regt is providing a popular entertainment feature in Holland these days. The entertainers claim they are strictly amateurs but the response form their mixed Canadian and Dutch audiences gives a much different indication. Under the direction of B.M. Russell, Auxiliary Services, they have established one of the finest entertainment centres in Holland. Included are M.S. LINKLATER (Halifax), CPL P.R. RUDDER (Toronto), F.J. YATES, (Fredericton), G.W. WRIDDEN (Truro), G.F. MORRIS (Carstairs, Alta), K.W. MURK (Tompkins, Sask.)

The "WESTERN GENTS" of "THE CHAPS" band of the Rainbow Review of the 5th Anti Tank Regiment. RCA, Loches, Holland. June 21, 1945.
(PA 136166 Photo by G.B. Gilroy)

FRONT LINE FOLLIES

Front Line Follies with Private J.C. Ducoin playing violin. Piedmonte, Italy, June 23, 1944 PA 152154 Photo by W.H. Agnew

ROYAL ALBERT HALL

Manager   REGINALD ASKEW.

HAROLD HOLT SUNDAY CONCERTS
SEASON 1941-42.

(Under the auspices of the Orchestral Concerts Society, Ltd.)

Sunday, April 19th, 1942, at 3

HAROLD HOLT presents

LONDON PHILHARMONIC
ORCHESTRA

Leader   REGINALD MORLEY

CONDUCTOR

DR. MALCOLM SARGENT

SOLOIST

SOLOMON

NO SMOKING

Programme and Notes 6d   Steinway Piano

SAISON 1944-1945

Mardi 17 avril 1945, à 19 h. 30

SONATES DE BEETHOVEN
DEUXIÈME CONCERT
PAR LE PIANISTE

Eduardo del PUEYO

PROGRAMME

1. Sonate en ut mineur, opus 10, n° 1.
   Allegro molto e con brio.
   Adagio molto.
   Finale (Prestissimo).

2. Sonate en ré majeur, opus 10, n° 3.
   Presto.
   Largo e mesto.
   Menuetto (allegro).
   Rondo (allegro).

— INTERRUPTION —

3. Sonate en fa majeur, opus 10, n° 2.
   Allegro.
   Allegretto.
   Finale (Presto).

4. Sonate en ré majeur, opus 28 (Pastorale).
   Allegro.
   Andante.
   Scherzo (allegro vivace).
   Rondo (allegro ma non troppo).

Piano S T E I N W A Y de la Maison H A N L E T

Les prochains concerts consacrés aux Sonates de Beethoven auront lieu les **mardis 24 avril, 1er, 8, 15, 22 et 29 mai 1945**, et commenceront à 19 h. 30 précises. Les portes seront fermées pendant l'exécution de chaque sonate.

PRIX : 5 Fr.

Some Programmes

NOT ONE OF YOUR REGULAR WAR TIME ENTERTAINERS.

"THE ZOOT SUIT"

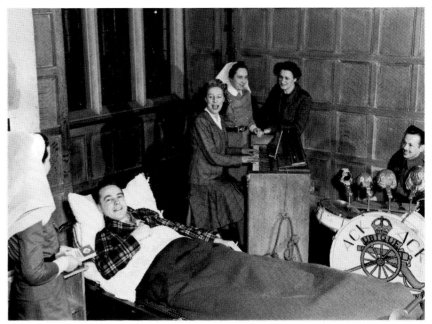

THE ACK-ACK ANNIE SHOW
Entertainment in hospital wards was most important but usually very small compact groups were better equipped for this work.

ACK-ACK ANNIE was one such unit. (Anti Aircraft - Ack-Ack)
Headed by Miss JUDY DOLLMAN on piano, the group is shown here providing songs and music for recuperating Major C.H./Jaimet of Hamilton, Ont.
#6 Casualty Clearing Station in England 1944.
Nursing Sister V.G. Coons of Dawson Creek, B.C., Judy Dollman, Nursing Sister K. Macleod of Kinross, P.E.I, Mrs. R. Needham, director of the show, and Cpl B. Lamarre of Longueil, Quebec on drums.
PA 176442 Photographer unknown

IN CONCLUSION

Since there are so many books about the Warriors of War, it is only reasonable from my point of view and experience, that I write about the Minstrels of War.

In doing so, the grim realities of the Second World War, or World War II, never for a moment escaped me and for that reason alone I wish to present the Stephens' family of five boys in the picture below.

I was the oldest and our sister, the youngest and I am eternally happy that at that time, there was no consideration made for the inclusion of women in active battle.

My contribution was not that of a Warrior. That passed me by.

Having spent ten years in the Canadian Army, with six of those overseas, (1936-1946) 'time' was my chief offering having arrived in England in December 1939 at the age of 23, and returned home to Canada in January 1946 at the age of 30.

My first two years were spent as a sergeant in the infantry (PPCLI) and Fate made all decisions. My last four years were with the bands in England, Italy, France, Belgium, Holland and Germany and a detailed story of that period appears in my book *THE HARPS OF WAR* (1986) which is now out of print being Canadian. My second book *MEMORIES AND MELODIES OF WORLD WAR II* also contains snippets of the same as well as 42 best known songs of World War II.

Now I present this composite picture of my brothers taken in London, England in June, 1944 shortly after "D" Day where three of us managed to show up and I have inserted the two missing brothers with the related tales of each.

Our father died in Regina at the age of 54 in the last week of May, 1944, just two weeks before "D" Day on June 6, 1944. My mother's father, a Boar War veteran had died several months earlier in Wales which was our birthplace.

It is difficult to comprehend the situation our mother in Regina, along with a young daughter, was left with.

THE PICTURE OF THE STEPHENS' BOYS

WILLIAM RAYMOND STEPHENS age 28 Extreme right (Author)
JAMES TAMPLYN STEPHENS age 24 Extreme left. Killed in action in Belgium. October 1944
BRYN STEPHENS age 22 Top insert. Could not appear because he was in action in France having landed in Normandy on "D" Day, June 6, 1944. When the war ended he was one of 26 from the Regiment (Regina Rifles) who survived.
SELWYN HENRY STEPHENS age 19 Centre in RCAF uniform. Was still on operational flights at this time and completed 40 missions in RCAF Bomber Command.

GODFREY BERNARD STEPHENS age 16 Bottom insert. Was already in uniform but because of his age he was refused overseas service.

DOCUMENTS

BANDS

HOW THE BANDS BEGAN

THE CANADIAN ARMY STAFF BANDS OVERSEAS 1940

FROM A. HAMILTON GAULT. Brigadier (PPCLI) Commanding "A" Group Holding Units. H.Q. "A" Groups I.F.H. Bordon Camp. Hants. England. Ref. Bands/1(A.G.1)

26 JULY 1940

"...reference to above mentioned letter it is considered...the reinstatement of Bands...will greatly add to the morale...of Canadian troops in England...

In 1938, the writer (Gault) selected a Bandmaster for the Princess Patricia's Canadian Light Infantry Band (Winnipeg)...L.A. Streeter, Kneller Haller Hall, England who was sent to Canada in August 1939...After outbreak of war September 3, 1939 the band was dispersed and Streeter left without duties...Suggest that Streeter be sent to England to organise the bands...

That the cost...for instruments...should be borne by me..."

Signed A. Hamiltin Gault.

Note: In 1914, Hamilton Gault, founded the famous PPCLI regiment in Ottawa out of his own funds.

FROM E.W. SANSOM Brigadier D.A.G. (Deputy Adjutant General) Canadian Military Headquarters. England

17 SEPTEMBER 1940

"During the present period of inactive ground warfare, special efforts be made to maintain morale...BANDS ARE CONSIDERED VERY VALUABLE AND ESSENTIAL...reform the bands...be authorised...One band for each holding unit with a total of nine...

Signed E.W. Sansom

FROM COLONEL W.B. WEDD Canadian Army Headquarters

TO SENIOR OFFICER Canadian Military Headquarters. 6/Bands/1 A.G.1

8 NOVEMBER 1940

"...authority now received for establishment of nine (later ten) bands...R.C.A. (Royal Canadian Artillery); R.C.E. (Engineers); R.C.S. (Signals); R.C.A.S.C. (Service Corps); R.C.A.M.C. (Medical Corps); 1st Infantry; 2nd Infantry; 3rd Infantry; 1st M.G. (Machine Gun). (In place of Medical and Machine Gun were R.C.O.C. (Ordnance) R.C.A.C. (Armoured); 4th Infantry.

...1 Bandmaster (W.O.1) and 27 bandsmen...taken from the ranks of units already serving overseas...

There is a suitable man from Canada, W.O.1 L.A. Streeter of the PPCLI...who has been kicked around in Winnipeg doing such menial jobs as raining buglers...He has...made himself disliked in Winnipeg but he is a "star turn and just the man we need..."

Signed W.B. Wedd

* * * * *

FROM CANMILITARY Ottawa

TO DEFENSOR England

8 NOVEMBER 1940

"...can probably obtain necessary bandmasters on loan from Kneller Hall (British Military School of Music)."

FROM V.W. ODLUM Major General Commanding 2nd Canadian Division

TO SENIOR OFFICER C.M.H.Q.

22 OCTOBER 1940

"...the (band) solution authorised does not begin to meet the need...I am not prepared to take action until I am sure full consideration has been given...A Holding Unit Band cannot be of great value to an active battalion...The greatest single service a band can give...is to revive the spirits on the last stages of a hard march...the esprit de corps...A Holding Unit band is nothing but a band...they (should) be so organized as to be easily divisible into sections suitable...as sub units...

Signed V.W. Odlum

FROM V.W. ODLUM Major General Commanding 2nd Canadian Division

TO MAJOR GENERAL MONTAGUE Senior Officer
  Canadian Military Headquarters

28 OCTOBER 1940
  "I have your (reference) October 24, 1940 in
  which you give me a lot of information I did not
  have before. IF GENERAL MCNAUGHTON
  HAS MADE A DECISION, I ACCEPT
  IT...nevertheless...the ordinary type of concert
  band is not what I...want...I would like to see
  music lighten the load of long marches...A band
  at the head of a columnhelps the head but does
  not do much good for the tail...I have done alot
  of long marches and have known the weariness
  under a heavy pack...what stirring band music
  does to heavy feet...
  Music applied at the right time and place can
  save a lot of drugs.
  Signed V.W. Odlum

FROM V.W. ODLUM Major General Commanding 2nd
  Canadian Division
TO LIEUT. GENERAL A.G. MCNAUGHTON
  Commanding Canadian 7th Corps
25 NOVEMBER 1940
  "...I am not thinking of bands for parade or
  concerts...I want bands to lift men at all times of
  physical depression and great strain as on long
  marches...only a band easily divisible into sub
  units will meet the need...at the time of great
  depression stirring march music has greater
  medicinal value than anything the doctors can
  give..."
  Signed V.W. Odlum

FROM P.J. MONTAGUE. Major General Senior
  Officer, C.M.H.Q.
TO MAJOR GENERAL ODLUM
2 DECEMBER 1940
  "It is no longer possible to use bands on marches
  because of the necessity of splitting columns
  into small groups...as protection from enemy
  aircraft...
  ...re...bands that are easily divisible...Brass bands
  do not lend themselves to such sub division...
  Signed P.J. Montague
Note: Major General Odlum was later removed form
command of the ill fated 2nd Division who went on the
catastrophe of Dieppe in August 1942. The General was
then sent to Australia as Canadian Ambassador. In 1943

he was transferred to China and later over to Turkey.

REGIMENTAL BANDS
18 NOVEMBER 1940
  Authority has now been received from Canada
  for the appointment of W.O.1 A.L. Streeter,
  PPCLI as Supervisor of Bands Overseas with
  the rank of Lieutenant, Director of Music...
  An official request has been forwarded to the
  War Office asking for the loan of up to 9 bandmasters from (The British Army)

DECEMBER 1940
  Initial purchase of 9 sets of instruments for
  band...It is strongly recommended that silver
  plated instruments be purchased...these can be
  easily and safely cleaned with soap and
  water...whereas...the brass finished instruments
  require constant treatment with polish that quickly
  deteriorates them, especially the soldering...
  Signed Colonel Wedd, CMHQ

FROM COLONEL W.B. WEDD A.G.1. C.M.H.Q. 6/
Bands/1
MEMORANDUM
7 DECEMBER 1940
  Lt. Streeter, supervisor of bands will probably
  turn up in a day or so...He arrived from Canada
  and it was thought that he was (a doctor) and so
  ended up in No 1 General Holding Unit with the
  Royal Canadian Army Medical Corp...
  BANDMASTERS...request forwarded to A.G.4
  for the loan of up to 9 bandmasters (British
  Army) The Treasury Department is pondering
  the situation...
  Signed W.B. Wedd

FROM L.F. PAGE Brigadier Commanding Base Units
18 MARCH 1941
  A band of 24 players is now functioning with the
  3rd Infantry Holding Division. (The 1st Infantry
  Division Band)...no flute or Eb clarinet players
  are available...

FROM MESSRS BOOSEY AND HAWKES LTD.
London, England
TO CAPT. A.L. STREETER Director of Canadian
Bands
6 MAY 1941
  ...we appreciated your broadcast on Monday
  afternoon...I was surprised at the excellence of

the band...since yo had said they were not quite the type you had in the British Army...How you managed to keep them in tune I do not know...Frank Wright (Musical Advisor to the BBC) said nice things about the same band which played in Trafalgar Square the week before. "Much above average" was his expression.

Signed W. Colbourne. Director B.H.

HEADQUARTERS CANADIAN REINFORCEMENT UNITS CRU 5-8
BROM BRIGADIER F.R. PHELAN Commanding Canadian Reinforcement Units
19 JANUARY 1942

The C.B.C. in conj8unction with the B.B.C...has a new series of band broadcasts...Programmes heard during the past 12 months (by unofficial Canadian Bands) leave much to be desired...Such broadcasts to be terminated and only official bands will be employed in future...

Signed F.R. Phelan

HEADQUARTERS, CANADIAN REINFORCEMENT UNITS
19 JANUARY 1942
CRU-5-8 Broad
F.R. PHELAN, BRIGADIER COMMANDER, Canadian Reinforcement Units

The Canadian Broadcasting Corporation, in conjunction with the British Broadcasting Corporation, is conducting a new series of band broadcasts...there is no standard demanded...on the unofficial (Canadian) bands. Programmes heard during the past 12 months...leave much to be desired.

Such broadcasts...to be terminated...(only) official bands will in future be employed...

HEADQUARTERS, CANADIAN REINFORCEMENT UNITS CRU-5-0-Bands
30 APRIL 1942
F.R. PHELAN, BRIG. C.R.U.

No. 1 Canadian Infantry Band has been able to function as an indepndent band...the RCA (Artillery) and the RCASC (Service) have been *'massed' to form a second band...*

Unable to meet demands for bands (due) to difficulty in obtaining musicians...

THE TWO *CANADIAN* BANDMASTERS ARE UNDER CONSTANT INSTRUCTION BY THE DIRECTOR OF MUSIC. (One was later

released (Garnett) and the other (Murphy) posted to the Armoured Corp band)

The band of THE *CANADIAN GRENADIER GUARDS*...may be expected for form the 2nd Canadian Infantry Band...

The band of the EDMONTON REGIMENT (16 Other Ranks) is being auditioned...

HEADQUARTERS C.R.U.
FROM BRIGADIER F.R. PHELAN C.R.U. Commander
30 APRIL 1942

Unable to meet the demands for bands (due) to the difficulty in obtaining musicians...Only 1st Canadian Infantry Band is able to function as an independent...The RCA (Artillery) and the RCASC (Service Corp) have been massed to form a second band.

The band of THE CANADIAN GRENADIER GUARDS (when it arrives from Canada) may be expected to form the 2nd Canadian Infantry Band. The regimental band of the Edmonton Regiment (16) is being auditioned.

1 JUNE 1942

The Canadian Armoured Corp band was able to commence work. Expected arrival of 2 more British bandmasters will...assist. Although no provisions were made for a dance band, each band is producing its own with music purchased (by the band members) and Knight of Columbus, Y.M.C.A. donating drum sets and 1 string bass. There is an increasing demand for the dance band.

9 JUNE 1942

...no misunderstanding...these official bands are for service with the Field units and are carried on strength of the Holding Units for training purposes only...They do not belong to any one formation and the Artillery band might be sent for duties to an infantry division...No flashes are permitted except Divisional.

Signed W.B. Wedd

MEMORANDUM TO A.G.7
4 JULY 1942

The 2nd Canadian Division has not had a band for several months...

(*19 AUGUST 1942* DIEPPE!!)

P.S. I have called Major Cote who advised me

that the 2nd Canadian Division will not require a band at this time...

FROM BANDMASTER BUCKMASTER 1st Canadian Infantry Band
23 AUGUST 1942 (four days after Dieppe)
"...a good deal of useful time has been wasted hanging around...attendance has been practically nil...no one knew the band was coming...I had to walk a mile to find a telephone box. It does not do good to keep men hanging about...please arrange the rest of the tour...to cheer up the band."

* * * * *

HEADQUARTERS CANADIAN REINFORCEMENT UNITS 499 Reports 1
SENIOR OFFICER C.M.H.Q.
3 JANUARY 1943
Canadian Corps Bands under organization
December 1942
No. 1 Canadian Infantry
No. 3 Canadian Infantry
Canadian Armoured Corp
R.C.A. (Artillery)
R.C.A.S.C. (Service Corp)
R.C.O.C. (Ordnance)
Signed F.R. Phelan, Brigadier

5TH CANADIAN MEDIUM REGIMENT R.C.A.
5CMR 6-4
Director of Music Canadian Army
20 APRIL 1943
The recent visit o the R.C.A. (Artillery) band to this unit under...Mr. Newman (bandmaster) was greatly appreciated... Unfortunately I did not see Mr. Newman...
Signed E.R. Suttle Lt/Col. 5th Med. RCA

UNDERSECRETARY OF STATE War Office, London, England
20 MAY 1943
British Bandmaster on Loan to Canadian Army

Buckmaster, F.	Cheshire Regiment
Hollick, A.R.	Northumberland Fusiliers
Newman, A.R.	3rd Kings Own Hussars
Keeling, D./	Seaforther
	Highlanders (Eng.)
Holt, C.A.	Royal Scots Greys
Hicks, L.H.	Black Watch
O'Conners, A.G.	A. and S.H.

HEADQUARTERS CANADIAN REINFORCEMENT UNITS (Overseas)
Senior Officer C.M.H.Q.
4 JUNE 1943
Engagements for May...Parades (80), Concerts (86), Church parades (27), Dances (57), Sports (5)
Total for one month 255
2 JULY 1943
Engagements for June...Parages (45), Concerts (111), Church (28), Dances (73), Sports (26)
Total for one month 283
4 AUGUST 1943
Engagements for July...Parades (56), Concerts (121), Church (17), Dances (69), Sports (33)
Total for one month 296
(signed) J.H. Roberts, Major General Commander Reinforcment Units.
(Note: Major General Roberts had commanded the illfated 2nd Division at Dieppe in August 1942 and was now relegated to Holding Unit on paper work.)

TO THE SECRETARY, DEPARTMENT OF NATIONAL DEFENCE Ottawa, Canada
From (Bandsman) J. MANNION, Preston, Ontario
30 OCTOBER 1943
"I wish to register...a complaint regarding the ...Canadian Bands overseas.
In November 1941 I was asked if I would go overseas and take charge of a band...On arrival...I found conditions existing did not warrant a chance...I don't know if you are aware...that no Canadian bandmasters are...in charge of the Canadian bands...I appealed to Captain Streeter (Director of Music Overseas), who told me *"THAT ALL CANADIAN BANDMASTERS SHOULD BE PUT AGAINST A WALL AND SHOT!"* and that..."...he would rather audition German bandmasters first!" I again appealed to this man Streeter who replied "It's no use, Mannion, None of these bands are going out...only under British bandmasters..." I said "very well, sir. I am going back to Canada."
Signed J. Mannion

CONFIDENTIAL CANADIAN BANDS OVERSEAS
FROM A.L. STREETER Director of Music
30 NOVEMBER 1943
"...I tested Mannion...his general knowledge was insufficient to employ as bandmaster...he admitted to this.
Mannion was a cornet player in the Canadian Armoured Corp band and later transferred to the Royal Canadian Artillery, then released to return to Canada.
British bandmasters had already been arranged for before I arrived in England. Such remarks...are obviously flights of imagination...It is impossible that any bandmaaster would pass such remarked to an ordinary member of his bands."
Signed A.L. Streeter, Captain D of M.

THE MAN CALLED STREETER

Author's note
Streeter, an Englishman, formerly of the 13th Hussars (India), bandmaster of the PPCLI (Winnipeg) and director of Canadian Army Bands overseas was indeed a controversial person if nothing else.

He was for his bands far beyond the call of duty. He would hurt and humiliate anyone who stood in his path bud had the good military sense to know where to treat softly. *"GET THESE DUMB GENERALS ON OUR SIDE AND WE'LL HAVE THE WHOLE BLOODY ARMY EATING OUT OF OUR HANDS."* As his sergeant for several years, the author saw the both sides of Streeter. He rode around like a military, Basil Rathbone, in a flag waving staff car from Army Headquarters, complete with driver who would open the door for Streeter to step out. He would then pause with hands behind his back and glare baleuflly around while timourous camp colonels peared perplexingly through office windows as to what manner of higher office had been dropped on them. The black arm band "D.M." was ominous until they realized, if ever, that it only stood for DIRECTOR OF MUSIC.

His range of bullet like, angry expressions knew no end. "MUSICIANS! I'VE SEEN BETTER CRAWL OUT OF CHEESE!" (Speaking of British rations, he was quite correct) "ALL CANADIAN BANDMASTERS SHOULD BE LINED UP AGAINST A WALL AND SHOT!" "I'LL HAVE YOUR BLOODY GUTS FOR GARTERS!" "YOU MARCH LIKE A BLOODY BUNCH OF C.W.A.C.'s (women) THE WRONG TIME OF THE MONTH!" then to me as band sergeant "THAT THAT HORRID TROMBONE PLAYER OUT AND

SHOOT HIM!" which of course I seldom did but had the poor wretch returned to his regiment where in due course, the enemy would perform the order.

He "demanded loyalty" but nevertheless, through his relentless and pitiless efforts he did create ten Canadian bands overseas the likes of which Canada had never known before and never will again.

W.Ray Stephens

DEPARTMENT OF NATIONAL DEFENCE ARMY, Ottawa
SENIOR OFFICER, C.M.H.Q. London, England
18 JANUARY 1944
...a situation in relation to...British bandmasters in the Canadian Army overseas...there is only one Canadian at the present time...
This...appears to warrant careful review...the public is very sensitive to this type of situation...where appointments in Canadian Army are not filled by Canadian Personnel...
Signed H.F.G. Letson, Major General
Adjutant General, Ottawa

Reply from Streeter
26 JANUARY 1944
The bands (Canadian) have reached their present standard of efficiency solely through the skilled training that has been available (British bandmasters)...The work demanded by the bands is such that they cannot avoid comparison to British Bands...
A.L. Streeter, D of M

CANADIAN ARMY BANDS MONTHLY REPORT
5 DECEMBER 1943
No. 1 Canadian Infantry Band and Canadian Armoured Corp Band proceeded to 7 Bn 2 CBRD for service in the Mediterranean Area November 21, 1943.
* * * * *

CANADIAN ARMOURED CORP BAND Mediterranean Theatre, North Africa
Report from Bandmaster P. Murphy (the sole Canadian)
23 JANUARY 1944
To Director of Music U.K.
Upon arrival in early December in Algiers (North Africa) it was discovered that nobody knew why

we had come or what we were to do...I was told...to proceed with band on S.S. Chantiles from North Africa to Sicily...After some hours on board we were suddenly ordered to disembark since there were over 400 troops too many on board...The band personnel left but by self and LCpl Mac Roberts stayed on board with the instruments.

Upon arrival at Catina (Sicily) we both had to unload then reload onto trucks and...went to Taomino 40 miles away...However it was 29 days before the rest of the band caught up with us and had to be flown from wher they had been stranded in Africa.

On the night of August 8, 1944, the dance band played at 7th Bn CBRD and a Lt/Col MacBeth wanted to sing with the band but no one could agree on a common key...the Colonel demonstrated his annoyance by throwing a glass of wine over the band after a certain response by one member of the dance group who was later removed from the band by this officer and sent off on duty...

Another time...5band replacements (due to sickness etc.) were intercepted and placed as guards ona mail train...It was 6 weeks before they turned up...

Signed P.P. Murphy, Bandmaster, C.A.C.

CANADIAN ARMY BANDS, Monthly Report
MARCH 1944

Bands were occupied in Army 2nd Corps and 4th Canadian Armoured Division. The R.C.A. (Artillery) bandparaded with Guard of Honour for H.M. The King at H.Q. 2nd Canadian Corps with General Montgomery 7 Bands proceeded to London for Military Tattoo in Hyde Park for "Salute the Saldier" week. 125,000 attended the parade.

19 MAY 1944

Distribution of bands will be as follows.
CANADIAN MEDITERRANEAN FROM
3 Bands
*WESTERN FRONT
5 Bands
UNITED KINGDOM
1 Band
(*This was prepared almost one month before "D" Day!)

Replacement of casualties must be considered. The old type of band work is dead...Bands needed to be versatile to entertain troops.

1 AUGUST 1944

Canadian Armoured Corp	Italy
No. 1 Infantry	Italy
R.C.C.S. (Signals)	Europe
No. 2 Infantry	Europe
No. 3 Infantry	Europe
R.C.A.S. (Service)	Italy
R.C.O.C. (Ordnance)	Europe
R.C.A. (Artillery)	C.M.H.Q. London
R.C.E. (Engineers)	United Kingdom
Total Strength	242

FROM BANDMASTER BUCKMASTER, 2nd Canadian Infantry Band
To Director of Music
28 SEPTEMBER 1944

"On the subject of my return to the British Army. Discipline in the band has been poor...I have tolerate...has rendered my position untenable and a great strain to my post as sole commander of a unit...a definite underground movement directed at me...fostered a spirit of hostility (which has) been unchecked before the N.C.A.'s and has injured both my prestige and my health...I have done all I could...an individual adopted a mutinous action...a counter attack against me...attitude of band hostile...rations were pilfered from a lorry...tapaulin torn to make air vent...and I am charged with starving the men... I must ask to be returned to the British Army...to retain my self respect...My conscience will not allow me to be party to an upheaval which will interfere with the prosecution of the War..."

Signed F. Buckmaster

FROM CAPTAIN A.L. STREETER, Director of Music
16 OCTOBER 1944

There has been trouble with this band since the day they arrived from Canada as the band of the Canadian Grenadier Guards in order to make the band of the 2nd Canadian Infantry Division.

I recommend that...bandmaster (Buckmaster)

be replaced and returned to the British Army...urgent...

Signed A.L. Streeter

TO SECRETARY OF NATIONAL DEFENCE,
Ottawa
21 NOVEMBER 1944

Bandmaster F. Buckmaster, Cheshire Regiment has recently been evacuated to hospital on medical grounds (neurological) and he should now be returned to British Army.

Signed P.J. Montague, Major General

CANADIAN ARMY BANDS, Monthly Report
1 NOVEMBER 1944

L/Sgt. F.M. McLeod to take charge of No. 4 Canadian Infantry Band.

FROM BANDMASTER HEMSTEAD, R.C.E.
(Engineers) Italy

"...must tell you that we 'requisitioned' a piano from under the hoses of the Jerry's (Germans) in Rimini...Went in town after dark and piano went downstairs within two minutes and onto truck before enemy had time to consider...Good piano too.

AND FROM ANOTHER BAND

"While playing a concert on a beach head for Canadians, two German 88's screamed overhead and exploded nearby sending troops scurrying for shelter. Band remained in position but did stop playing. Bandmaster swore out loud "F... THE BLOODY GERMANS! WE'LL SHOW THE BASTARDS!" and the band played "God Save the King" as loud as possible.

CANADIAN ARMY BANDS, General Report
7 FEBRUARY 1945

Recommend that the Director of Music, Captain Streeter, be sent to the 21st Army H.Q. for a visit...fatigue and exhaustion of band personnel is of concern...They have no central area of administration, medical care of unit support...The conditions under which these mobile bands have been playing is serious...

AUXILLIARY SERVICES ENTERTAINMENT UNITS
8 FEBRUARY 1945

Major A.L. Streeter, Director of Music, Bands and Major R. Purdy, Director of Concert Parties,

agreed upon the mutual problem of obtaining musicians from drafts from Canada...

With the end of the war in sight, many of the original bandsmen and performers, from as early as 1939, will be returning home...

Signed C.S. Booth, Brigadier

17 MARCH 1945

The time will...arrive shortly when 8 bands will be needed in the theatre (Europe) of operations...Instead of maintaining the high standards that 4 years of hard work has produced the bands will be deteriorating through leave to Canada...

Signed K.G. Blackadier, Brigadier
(Note: All band personnel were 'frozen' in Europe for as long as 9 to 10 months after war ended.)

8 MAY 1945 THE WAR OFFICIALLY ENDED IN EUROPE

SOLDIER CONCERT PARTIES

In 1941, the creation of the Soldier Concert Parties began.

CBU-5-Aux.12-6
S/CAPT. AUXILIARY SERVICES
CANADIAN ENTERTAINMENT BROADCAST
15 JANUARY 1941

"In response to your request of January 13, 1941, I proceeded to the Criterian Theatre, London...with a party of one officer and 12 Other Ranks...to broadcast...

...broadcast was as follows...(involved were BERT CHURCHILL, R. JORDON, LIET. H. FAIR, W. MOSKALYK, MCLEAN, LOU HOOPER, N. PYRAH, with songs composed and arranged by A.D. MCCRINDLE, Supervisor Canadian Legion War Services.)

...C.B.C. announcer GERRY WILMOT, (Canadian War Correspondent) (was) very pleased with the programme provided by the Holding Units...

All participants were accommodated in the Theatre for sleeping purposes, matressed and blankets being provided...

Signed A.D. McCrindle

Author's note: The first actual broadcast was as early at Feb. 1940 when a group of twenty vocalists were selected from the 1st Division to open the first Canadian Hostel in London. During the long trip by bus we were rehearsed until exhausted on "ROLL OUT THE BARREL", "WE'RE GOING TO HANG OUT THE WASHING" and "WE'RE ON OUR WAY TO BERCHTESGADEN" by the composer of the latter, Hermann Darowski.

R.G. Vol 16, 664
ASSISTANT DIRECTOR AUXILIARY SERVICES,
C.M.H.Q.
20 MARCH 1941

Item #8 ENTERTAINMENT
"...it was felt that steps should be taken to expedite the formulation of Army (Soldier) Concert Parties...(England)
* * * * *

CANADIAN AUXILIARY SERVICES
30 APRIL 1941

Item #14 Soldier Concert Parties
"...approval has been given to assemble a small group of one Headquarters section of 5 Other Ranks and two parties of 16 Other Ranks as Base Units for training and availability to Field Formations when ready...

MINUTES OF THE MEETING HELD IN THE OFFICE OF THE ASSISTANT DIRECTOR AUXILIARY SERVICES, 17 Cockspur St., London, S.W.1 at 1100 hours 5 May 1941.
5 MAY 1941
The following were present:

MAJOR J.M. HUMPHREY	Assistant Director Auxiliary Services
CAPT. E.D. OTTER	Canadian Y.M.C.A. Overseas
BRIG. T.H. MUNDAY	Salvation Army Can. War Services
COLONEL W. RAE	Canadian Legion War Services
MR. W.T. SLADE	Knights of Columbus Army Units

3 ENTERTAINMENT
Col. Rae stated that the Legion had been faced with unexpected drains due to having to employ *professional concert parties*...It has been understood that *SOLDIER CONCERT PARTIES*...were to be the principal forms of entertainment...permission from the Army was not obtainable...professional parties had to be used...(and paid for)...(these paid) parties should be reduced...the whole field of entertainment be viewed in the light of...*SOLDIER CONCERT PARTIES*...

...The Y.M.C.A. and the Knights of Columbus expressed desire to be responsible for supporting *one each* of these...It was emphasized that the soldiers should be encouraged to display their talents...and that soldier concert parties...be throughout the Canadian Forces Overseas...

...it was agreed upon...be desirable to abolish professional parties...
AUDITIONS
...it was announced that owing the *SUPERVSOR N.W. PLUNKETT'S* illness...Supervisor F.C. ANDERS was to take over the work...of soldier auditions...
(*Morton Wesley Plunkett. Creator and director

of World War I Canadian "Dumbells in France."
Went overseas in World War II to continue his
work but returned to Canada due to illness.)
CINEMAS
...Major Humphrey...discovered that some units
were having as many as three show changes per
week..He said, two shows a week was adequate...

MEETING OF AUXILIARY SERVICE CORPS
15 MAY 1941
...the present aim was to have four soldier con-
cert parties in action by 1st SEPTEMBER|1941...
After due deliberation...the following...needs
were given...

CORPS TROOPS	2 Parties
1ST DIVISION	2 Parties
2ND DIVISION	3 Parties
BASE UNITS	2 Parties.

* * * * *

ASSISTANT DIRECTOR AUXILIARY SERVICES
20 MAY 1941
"During a visit to ADAS, Supervisor Anders and
Sgt. S. Sheddon, stated their difficulty in getting
permission in certain cases from Commanding
Officers to hold auditions because of fear that
men *will be taken* away *from them...*ADAS
advised them to *stress* to the Commanding Officers the need for entertainment and that they
would not necessarily be loosing their men..."

MEETING OF THE ENTERTAINMENT
COMMITTEE
4 SEPTEMBER 1941
PIANOS...complaints were reported regarding
the condition of pianos available...complaints
had also been received of "ladies" (ENSA) being
transported in open back trucks...*suggested that
rugs be provided...*
*NAME FOR SOLDIER CONCERT PARTIES...*it
was felt... decision should be made...on a name
for the Soldier Concert Parties...
WORKING HOURS...it was agreed that soldier
concert parties should not work more than six
days a week...(nothing about three shows a day!)
11 SEPTEMBER 1941
The presence of Capt McLaws offered the opportunity for asking about the complaint...about
dressing rooms in No. 3 L.H.U...Capt McLaws
was ignorant of any complaints...

SOLDIER CONCERT PARTIES
The first performance at Canadian Base Units on
September 8th was a definite success...clipping
from the (London) Evening News...was read out
amid general approval...(It) was cited that a
Senior OFficer formerly against (concert parties) had been won over by the first performance...
DIFFICULTIES OF TROOP MOVEMENTS
It was stated troop movements had
*interfered...*with schedules of concert
parties...Capt McLaws added his voice... spare
concert *parties thrust upon* him because of his
stationary base unit...
It was pointed out that Concert Parties *were
never thrust upon anybody...they were
offered...*He (McLaws) was then asked what
opinion of his Formation Concert Party
Committee...Capt McLaws (Canadian Base
Units) professed complete ignorance...McLaws
was of the opinion that any one man could
handle such affairs...He was...told...that the plan
worked well throughout the Canadian army and
that (he) should act unquestionably upon an
order such given...
A motion was then passed that in future Concert
Parties will be made available *only through the
Formation Concert Party Committee...*Capt.
McLaws voiced his objection...

* * * * *

*MINUTES OF MEETING OF ENTERTAINMENT
ADVISORY COMMITTEE HELD AT THE OFFICE
OF THE CANADIAN Y.M.C.A. LONDON,
ENGLAND*
2 OCTOBER 1941
SOLDIER CONCERT PARTY Ambassadors
Theatre, 9 October 1941
It was agreed that the "*TIN HATS*" should given
their London showing at (the above theatre)...it
was decided to give two shows...same day...
The first show should be for Other Ranks, the
female civilian staff of C.M.H.Q...
The second show for the Officers and *important
people...*the High Commissioner for Canada
Vincent Massey and his wife...etc., etc., ...
It was decided that the *M.P.'s (Military Police)
should be present for the (Other Rank) show to
preserve law and order...Ushers only* should be
provided for *the (second) show with special
attention paid to the...Dress Circle...*

It was suggested...to report...covering the following points..."Outlining the difficulties of *late hours* and the *unwillingness of* the (show) men to *get up early*...
"...that men of the Soldiers Concert Party when stopped by the M.P.'s (Military Police)...for not having passes...

FIRST PERFORMANCE BY THE TIN HATS
9 OCTOBER 1941

"It depressed us both (wife) and we were entirely disingenuous in offering congratulations to the company at its conclusion." Statement by High Commissioner to England, *VINCENT MASSEY.* (Massey however *was always known to judge by rank and wealth* rather than talent.)
RAYMOND MASSEY, film actor and brother of Vincent, came to Canada early in the war to add support to the entertainment efforts...he was given a 'paper pushing' job in Ottawa and became so angry that he left to return to the U.S.A. where he immediately took out American citizenship papers...

* * * * *

The Professional Shows of Britain known as E.N.S.A. (Entertainment National Service Association) were very much disliked by Canadians, most of whom had never been introduced to the vulgar English music halls...Their (Canadian) only entertainment back home being Saturday night at the Bijou watching Dick Powell in "Goldiggers of 1933" or the occasional 'farmer's daughter' joke.
"I am not satisfied with the type of show that E.N.S.A. is giving which from my own experience...is quite vulgar..." Gen. McNaughton. Other reports..."*One of the poorest shows ever seen...the foulest...filthy dirty jokes...and then THEY CAME TO THE OFFICERS MESS AFTER!"*

WAR DIARY
Auxiliary Services C.M.H.Q.
18 OCTOBER 1941

...necessity of providing suitable accomodation for the Soldier Concert Party, TIN HATS, ...stated that...a few of the members are called upon to be in 'good voice' nightly...and...health and comfort requires...consideration...(even though) the cast is made up entirely of 'soldiers'...there should

be some preferred treatment...in 5 days of October 1941 (13th to 17th) the Tin Hats played to over 2,000 Canadian troops...

* * * * *

MEETING OF THE ENTERTAINMENTS ADVISORY COMMITTEES
5 FEBRUARY 1942

...the reception and accommodation of the *TIN HATS* on the RAF stations visited were...in some cases...non existent...
Transportation constantly broke down...illness broke out among the company...six were sent to hospital...noted that this was the worst weather in England...for 31 years...

Capt. Boucher pointed out that *all members of the SOLDIER CONCERT PARTIES would have to revert to the rank of Private within one week, or else removed...*
...in view of the success...achieved by THE TIN HATS and THE KIT BAGS...consideration be given...for trades pay...*a special allowance of $.50 per day be paid by the Auxiliary Service Organizations...ATTENDANCE to KIT BAG shows for 5 days* (Jan 19-23) 2,400

* * * * *

ASSISTANT DIRECTOR AUXILIARY SERVICES WAR DIARY
MAY 1942

"...consistent reports indicate the soldier concert parties, TIN HATS and KIT BAGS were the most popular shows..."

MEETING OF THE ENTERTAINMENTS ADVISORY COMMITTEE
18 JUNE 1942

...the *performance of the TIN HATS at Wyndahm's Theatre on the 15th was a great success*...however several complaints were received about the behaviour of the party...
...*No transport* had been arranged to move the party to London
...*Hot dinner* was ordered for 28 men...only 8 turned up to eat.
...*Hot supper* after show was ordered for 14 men...3 turned up...
...*Beds for the night* were booked in a Canadian Y.M.C.A. and out of 14 reserved only 12 were occupied...*One of the men went to bed in full*

uniform and boots resulting in the bed being ruined and the room unusable for 48 hours.

It was agreed (by the committed) that this was the result of poor administration by the Officer in charge...*Capt. Poulter left the meeting...*

* * * * *

Mr. Anders advised...that the 3rd Soldier Concert Party would be ready to go on the road in about one week...

...Officers in charge of the Soldiers Concert Parties were being changed immediately...New officers would be appointed...and given a list...of duties etc.

...permission for TIN HATS to visit Winchester...this was refused for several reason, one being The Copyright Performing Society.

...a request from H.Q. United States Army (England) for use of TIN HATS...was refused...

...The large ENSA Concert parties be dropped...end of the month...

...KIT BAGS returned from tour of RCAF and Canadian Forestry Corp.

...discussion of one account for 5.8.6d for various tools required for repairs and construction on Tin Hats equipment... approved...

No. 3 Det (Tin-Hats)
5 AUGUST 1944

INCIDENT INVOLVING NO. 3 DET (TIN HATS) SERIAL 22547C/1

1.   On Monday, 24 July 1944, the m/n Det. embarked on the SS "Empire Beatrice" (MTT S-333) en route to Normandy. After waiting in the Thames Estuary for the convoy to assemble, the ship eventually sailed in convoy at approx 1430 hrs Wednesday, 26 July 1944...On board ship the personnel had been detailed to lifeboats and rafts, and lifeboat drill and action station drill had been held several times. Everyone was conversant with the action to be taken incase of trouble.

2.   At approx. 2333359 hrs, 26 July 1944, gunfire was heard from the Naval escort, and at the same time the Air Force was shooting down flying-bombs overhead. The noise from both sources kept everyone awake. It was learned later that the ship had received an E-boat warning at approx. midnight. At approx 0045 hrs the action-station alarm was sounded from the bridge of the ship but, due to the terrific noise, it was not heard by the majority of the personnel on board. An officer was sent from the bridge to notify (by word of mouth) the personnel of this alarm.

3.   All the Tin Hats personnel were quartered in the aft hold of the ship. M-15979 A/Cpl Rocks J. luckily heard the alarm and immediately ordered all personnel to stand by their beds and close to the side of the ship. This was undoubtedly responsible for the saving of a number of lives.

4.   Before the officer mentioned above could reach the men's quarters, the ship was hit by a star shell - evidently fired by an E-boat. In another few minutes the ship was hit by a torpedo, in the stern just aft of the men's quarters. Lifeboat stations were immediately called but, due to the damage by the torpedo, the rafts in the stern were not available. Personnel detailed to these rafts were sent forward to other lifeboats and rafts, which finally caused considerable overcrowding.

5.   At the time of the explosion, the stairways from the hold to deck collapsed; the floor where the men's beds were also collapsed. The fact that the majority of the men were standing near the sides saved nearly everyone from falling into the hold and the bottom of the ship. Several did fall through but managed to scramble to safety. K-75470 Pte VanBuskirk H was pinned in the hole by debris and was rescued by G-52551 Pte Cormier A.J. Ptes Harper, Phillips and Miskelly all fell through but eventually reached the deck. The personnel left the ship by raft and lifeboat.

6.   One lifeboat (badly overcrowded) and containing about twelve members of the Party was leaking badly; it was kept above water by men bailing the water out with tin-hats and working the pump. A/Cpl Rocks was a spirited member in this boat and his singing was a steadying influence on the personnel in the boat who were very near panic. Survivors in this boat and some rafts were picked up by a Naval MB and taken to Dover harbour, arriving at about 0530 hrs. This included Ptes Miskelly, Harper, VanBuskirk and Beaudoin who were all injured. There were no complaints from anyone. Injured personnel were immediately taken to Dover County Hospital. Other personnel were landed at Folkestone by the Pilot Tender at approx. 1015 hrs.

7.   Uninjured personnel who landed at Dover were taken to the South Front Bks (2nd Bn 7th Royal Warwicks) where everyone had breakfast, a hot bath and given a bed. (The personnel who landed at Folkestone caught up with the Party in the afternoon.

8.   From this action the following other ranks are missing (killed).

B-77	Tpr	Bendit	J
G-45058	Pte	MacDonald	B H
B-67280	A/Sgt	More	C
K-16058	Gnr	Renney	J D

P-9268   Gnr   Witherall   A
(Sgt More and Gnr Witherall were seen on deck, they were later killed.)

9. The survivors in one of the ship's lifeboats were taken to France, but no word has been received as yet if any of the missing personnel were amongst their numbers.

10. The ship itself did NOT sink; it will be towed to port and unloaded, after the necessary repairs for this action have been completed.

WAR DIARY
FEBRUARY 1945

During the month of February...realization that a solution be found...for Canadian productions of new entertainment groups for service in battle zones...Canad will dispatch one show per month...so far out of five sent...none are ready to perform...necessary to weed out personnel...disposing of unsatisfactory surplus... Arriving...are CWAC volunteers who are not matched for size...who are not attractive...and unable to dance...perhaps these girls are not convinced of the proper soldiery attitude...Though appearance of male personnel in entertainment groups is not an important requirement as in the case of the CWAC's not a great deal can be said in favour of this sex (male)...they have a low talent content and their keeness of military attitude is NOT very sharp...Costumes too, are a headache...Comedy material is poor...soldiers in the field appreciate good, clean comedy...as produced in the original five groups (SOLDIER CONCERT PARTIES)...arrived in 1943...Troops who have been overseas for five years...have little interest in "recruiting skits!"...

This month the following (original) groups were distributed as follows:

21st Army Europ	"KIT BAGS"
	"BANDOLIERS"
	"FORAGE CAPS"
	"RAPIDFIRE"
Mediterranean Forces	"OFF THE RECORD"
	"ABOUT TURN"
	"HAVER-SACKS"
U.K. for reconditioning	"FUNBORNE FOLLIES"
	"MUSICAL MANOEUVRES"
U.K.	"COMBINED OPS"
	"THE FLOOR SHOW"
Canada	"INVASION REVUE"
	"TIN HATS"

RG24 Vol 16.1672 File 2636/1

WAR DIARY
26 FEBRUARY 1945

DOUG ROMAINE...comic is now with "THE FLOOR SHOW" an Army Show Hospital Entertainment Unit...

"KIT BAGS" now known as "No. 10 Det. Aux. Service Entertainment Unit".

Major W.V. George, Assistant Director Auxiliary Services C.M.H.Q. left for Canada today...entertainment groups arriving from Canada are of such low calibre and...unsuitable for presentation in the field...he has to go back to see what can be done..."

11 APRIL 1944

In view of the large numbers of personnel...leaving the "FORAGE CAPS" for Canada...not to rebuild this show but post to other groups...

B82960 Pte CROUTER W.C. of the "FUNBOURNE FOLLIES" was married.

18 APRIL 1945

C6048 A/Sgt Abrum L.G. of "FORAGE CAPS" posted to H.Q. ...employed as Sgt. in charge of Social Entertainment...

30 APRIL 1945

D1555531 A/Cpl DOUCET (Roger) vocalist of a "RAPID FIRE" group was despatched to the Broadcast Unit in London, England...

APRIL 1944

As the month of April drew to a close there were 7 entertainment groups at Base and one on leave...

"ABOUT TURN" group is waiting privilege leave in U.K. ...some delay has occurred...show equipment and personal kit belonging to CWAC personnel...has been lost...appears to be scattered...from point of embarkation in Europe to docks in U.K. and *possibly may be in a railway van waiting to be unloaded...*

"FORAGE CAPS" on general duties in Camp Area...future somewhat uncertain...majority of entertainers from this group arrived overseas in 1939...are due to leave for Canada...may shelve this show in its entirety...

"MUSICAL MANOEUVRES" now called "SWING PATROL" prepared to go to Europe... "RAPID FIRE" Group is...on general fatigue duties... "PLAY PARADE" Group...prepaired also for Europe...

"OFF THE R|ECORD" group...standing by...

"THE FLOOR SHOW"...the little bundle of mirth and melody...in entertaining hospitals in U.K.

...with Victory around the corner there will be a great increase for entertainment for Canadian forces in this continent...

WAR DIARY   The Canadian Army Shows
1 MAY 1945

Inspection parade of all personnel at 0815 hours...

...due to the missing equipment of the CWAC's...they are at present wearing battle dress because all tunics are in their kit bags...

...this evening RTO (Railway Military Personnel) advised that some of the equipment had been located in a railway van at Aldershot siding...no personal gear however...

"MUSICAL MANOEUVRES" recently re designated as "SWING PATROL" because it is felt a wise policy to (change) names so that the troops (will think it is a new show)...

Three personnel of "FUNBORNE FOLLIES" were despatched to London...to appear as guests of a programme broadcast tomorrow at 1700 hrs. These are A/Br. Greisman; A.Bd Lovett: (Comedians) *Pte Crouter W., vocalist.*

Male personnel of "RAPID FIRE" were employed today on fatigue duties around the barracks...

W. Pte Clendinning CWAC is recovering from an attack of pneumonia...Civilian piano tuner from Guildford employed today...

WAR DIARY Canadian Auxiliary Services
(*Note: This is not your usual War Diary, but whoever wrote it evidently was an ardent writer)
7 MAY 1944

Fatigues again for the male members of "RAPID FIRE"...CWAC's rehearsed dance routine...

In spite of work and rehearsals this morning and afternoon, there seemed to be a feeling experienced by every member of the Unit that there was something in the wind...that we were on the

Eve of great news...Conversations between rest periods and breaks in rehearsals turned to the topic of the day...V.E. DAY...

News reports over the BBC found personnel huddling around loudspeakers...in Camp...The Officer Commanding etc were no exceptions and at 1400 hrs they called together the various heads of departments of the Units to discuss preparations for celebrating VICTORY DAY... The usual sight which greets one's eye upon entering the Camp Area, is a quiet adn serene picture of a large English estate...sweeping landws of green grass extending in every direction with an occasional soldier in CWAC in Khaki, walking either to or from rehearasal halls...

At 1700 hrs...Prime Minister Winston Churchill was expected to make an announcement...that the people of the Empire had waited to hear almost six years of "blood, sweat and tears" to borrow the English "Bulldogs'" own words...quantity of beer...had been waiting in the messes for almost a week...Volunteers were at the alert beside the taps with bottle openers in hand...

At 1800 hrs rain began to fall...*at 2000 HOURS THE BBC ANNOUNCED THAT TOMORROW MAY 8, 1944, WOULD BE VICTORY DAY IN EUROPE...*

"Let's throw out O.C. in the Fountain" someone yelled...but no one did

"Let's throw the B.S.M. in the fountain" someone shouted. So they did.

..."SWING PATROL" performed at No. 1CRU (Cove) and returned at 2330 hours but were too tired to join in the celebration and went to bed...

CANADIAN REINFORCEMENT UNITS
Officer Commanding, Canadian Army SHow
9 MAY 1944

Would express to Sgt Abrum and the orchestra of the Army Show...for the V.E. Ball at H.Q.C.R.U. on Tuesday night...

...it is even more appreciated because...their sacrifce of their own evening to provide entertainment.

Signed B.W. McLean Major

CONCERT PARTY MANAGER'S REPORT
"FIVE HITS AND A MISS"
21 MAY 1945

Monday	Hospital Ward	Show well received
Tuesday	Hospital Ward	3 wards... well received
Wednesday	Hospital Ward	Mild eception wards were bone cases...90% of patients on back

Etc.

The Canadian Legion Supervisor, Mr. A.E. Mourant...was not very co-operative...took everything for granted...I asked for a trolley to move a piano...he told me to go look for one...He was not interested but his staff were helpful...

Worried about the V.D. wards...Do we play them with CWAC personnel?

Cpl Grant N.C.O.

Reply from Can. Aux.

...True enough that patients received their "wounds" (V.D.) "in action" and it is impossible to entertain them outside their wards...but one hesitates to send female entertainers to these wards...The Commanding Officer authorizes the *EXCLUSION of* CWAC personnel from performances of "duties" therein...

WAR DIARY

23 MAY 1944   Guildford, Surrey

...Pte St. John-Simpson, G.S. ...to London to procure costumes and supplies for show "APRES LA GUERRE" Group...

Routine dances, fan dance, skits and vocal selections... rehearsed...for "APRES LA GUERRE"...

Conference was called by the Officer Commanding included Major R.J. Purdy, Lt. V. Sweeny (CWAC), Ltd. W.E. Sandburn, C.M.S.J.E. Hozack, CSM A.A. Bradanovich, Sgt H.M. Gill, C.S.M.R.M. Burns...

The WAR DIARIST sat in on the Conference...in order to give *historians* some idea of the many duties involved...

Music for "DON'T FORGET THE GIRLS" ACT has been completed...

Music for "THE TAP TRIO" now being scored...

Two pianos are taken on...stools are being built by the carpenter shop...

24 MAY 1944

Innoculation parade at 0815 hours

12 JUNE 1945

Jimmy Coxon posted to "MIXED FUN" today...

More shows being named:

"WARD HEALERS" (not for V.D. Wards) "HAM 'N' LEGS" "OPS-A-DAISY" "PLAY PARADE" "ABOUT TURNS"

ENSA shows now attached to Canadian Army: "GET TOGETHER" "ROTTERS" "MUSIC AND MAGIC" "ALEWYCH" "GAIETY" "DOUBLE SCOTCH" "BIG BEN" "WAIT FOR IT" "JOY STICKS" "FOG LAMPS" "SUN RAYS"

RCAF

SUMMARY TO: WAR COMMITTEE OF THE
CABINET (CANADA)

H.Q./54.-27-12-64-Vol 2.
OCT. 27, 1942 "The Army Show (Canada)"
Re: Formation of Concert Party to be Known as "The Army Show" and to Consist of Army Personnel

PURPOSE:
This proposal concerns the organization of the Radio-Theatrical Party from Army personnel...The main objectives are:
(a) Provision of a new medium for recruiting
(b) Additional favourable contact between Army and potential recruits
(c) Increase public and Army morale.

PERSONNEL:
9 Officers and 71 Other Ranks.
Temporary civilian assistance...leading well known performers will be employed...

EXPERIENCE IN THE UNITED STATES
Precedents for this type of recruiting and moral activity exist in the U.S.A. where (they) have 39 such shows already formed...Best known...is "*THIS IS THE ARMY*" directed by IRVING BERLIN...

PROCEDURE AND PROGRAMME
Formation of personnel early Nov. 1942
Rehearasals during November
Radio broadcasts beginning December 1942
Stage presentations...early 1943

PROPOSAL HAS BEEN RECOMMENDED BY
Minister of National Defence
National Recruiting Campagin
Chief of General Staff
D.M. Army for financial aspects

DEPARTMENT OF NATIONAL DEFENCE ARMY
H.Q.54-27-12-64 DAR 1a)
Meeting in connection with ARMY SHOW...office of *Mr. Victor George* Whitehall Broadcasting Ltd.., Montreal.
Oct. 29, 1942 Ottawa
PRESENT

Mr. Victor George, Chairman
Lt/Col James Mess
Mr. Jack Arthur
Mr. Geoffrey Waddington
Mr. Rai Purdy
Major W.B. Robinson
Capt. J.K. Reid
Mr. Edward Harris
Mr. John Partt

TRADES PAY
...is causing Mr. George some concern...highly qualified musicians and performers...entitled to pay *considerably higher* than that of an *ordinary bandsman*...($.25 extra per day)...It was suggested for the time being, *it be $.50 extra per day*...

TRANSPORTATION (In Montreal)
...suggested that personnel might use Army trucks...Mr. George considered this *unfair*...particularly in cold weather...to transport musicians (thusly) and expect their hands to be in sufficient...condition to rehearse...

DANCE INSTRUCTION
...Jack Arthur stated that the services of a dance master...such as Bob Alton...from New York be obtained.
Mr. Hume Cronyn, Canadian actor in Hollywood, offered his services to the Army Show...suggested he be offered an "advisory capacity" ona volunteer basis...
Mr. Robert Farnum...as Chief Arranger.
The Army Show...Is Intended to be...A Unit of the Canadian Army...with sub units under its direction.

Potential executives...(Officers) with sufficiently high educational and physical qualifications...for O.T.C. (Officers' Training) when time for training permits...Economical conditions do not present difficulties...*granting the patriotic zeal*...of the participants...

4 NOVEMBER 1942
TRAINING AND QUALIFICATIONS FOR ARMY SHOW OFFICERS...will be required to pass a special one month course at Borden or Brockville...
OTHER RANKS...will be required to undergo the complete Basic training course...All ranks on strength of The Army Show...will be available for military training each morning up to 1200 hours.
...there will be no interference or change of plan in this matter. *Some equipment such as Bren guns will be required...which are not normally in use in the mornings by the Reserve Forces...*

(signed) *Ernest G. Weeks, Brigadier*

DRILL SYLLABUS FOR OTHER RANKS OF THE ARMY
SHOW*
20 NOVEMBER 1942

Position of Attention
Formation of Squad in Threes
Dressing and Numbering
Marching in Quick Time
Marking Time

Side Stepping and Recapitulation
Turning on the March
Changing Direction

Lecture on War gases
The Army Act Lecture
Route March

Drill...At Ease...Right Turn...LeftTurn...About
     Turn...
Saluting...to the Front...to the Left...the
     Right...Without Arms...
Respirator Drill...Slung...Alert...Alternative
     Alert...
Route March...with particular attention to march
     discipline...
(*You're In the Army Now!)

ARMY SHOW

ARMY SHOW

The Army Show is under the command of *Major W.V. George.*

Producer will be Capt. (later Lt/Col) *Raj Purdy*

Musical Director *Capt Geoffrey Waddington*

Mr. Jack Arthur will serve in advisory capacity

A/Sgt Lisa Lineaweaver will be in command of the C.W.A.C.'s after completing qualifying course.

Robert Farnon will be taken of until his present radio contract ends...as Captain.

...Only top ranking talent will be accepted for The Army Show for it is to be Canada's Soldier Show and must be of the highest claibre...

(...and so they come) *Nov. 14th* two pianos...*Nov 17th* Transport failed to get men to studio for first rehearsal...*Nov. 18th* Other Ranks spent morning cleaning barracks...*Nov. 20th* Major W.V. George was in uniform...*Nov. 21st* 20 Other Ranks arrived...*Nov. 22nd* Capt. Wren spent the day in Toronto...*Nov. 23rd* Private Frank Shuster arrived...*Nov. 26th*...Private Rockwood arrived today...4 men sick with colds...Arrival of C.W.A.C.'s next week...no quarters available...*Nov. 27th*...Squad seen at drill...*Nov. 28th*...Dress rehearsal...not sufficient sopranos and altos...*Nov. 30th*...wire from Jimmie Shields arriving soon...

Sunday December 13th 1942

First broadcast over C.B.C. Radio.

From C.S. Booth. Brigadier. D.A.G. Can. Military Headquarters

ROYAL CANADIAN ARTILLERY BAND, London Broadcasting Unit *29 SEPTEMBER 1944*

...The Entertainment Unit. (Robert Farnon) has now arrived in the U.K. to provide Canadian radio programmes for the AEFF Broadcast...

...The RCA (Artillery) band can now be released...for normal duties...

...certain commitments...however...have been made and they cannot be fully released until 10 Oct. 1944...

The band can then be dispatched to Italy on the next convoy...

DIRECTORATE OF INFORMATION
17 APRIL 1942

The Royal Canadian Air Force Revue "*BLACKOUTS*" has started from *Ottawa* to tour stations *throughout Canada*

...strictly for RCAF personnel...produced, directed and presented by members of the RCAF. It includes a "*lissome*" (lithesome) chorus from the Women's Division (W.D.)...The unit is a compact group...from the ranks...for entertainment at stations...where *off duty amusement is a problem*...Includes a 12 piece band...Another unit may be formed at a later date.

The unit is so versatile that the entire cast consists of only 32 young men and women...they give the impression of a much larger company. Producer is Squadron Leader *Norman Gilchrist,* Director of Music for the RCAF...along with F/L *Robert Coote*, F/L *Bryant Fryer*, F/L *Wishart Campbell* and Section Officer *Lola Thompson,* dance instructress. Stage manager is Cpl *Terry Dowding*, comedy gags by LAC *Sam Levine. etc...*

All music was arranged by Cpls *Ken Bray* and *Morry Hyman.* Indications are that they'll make the Air Force men and women '*happier*' in the *Service.*

FROM: R.1608556 A.C. Bray

TO: *F/l D. Lusk, Officer Commanding.*
        No. 16 Service Flying School,
        Hagersville, Ontario

27 NOVEMBER 1942

...that the RCAF is holding auditions...in Ottawa...forming a Concert Party for the RCAF...

...I would be more of an asset...in such work...appeared in The "Theatre Under the Stars (Van)"...baritone lead in "Merrie England" "Mikado" "Belle of New York"...I have been in radio shows in every city in Canada...In 1939-40 I was with the Imperial Three Star Entertainers...under Capt. F. Anders...(of the Canadian Legion Services in Englnad)...I was organist and choir master in Shelton Memorial Church in Vancouver...also taught, and did further radio and club work...While enlisting in Calgary I sang...with the Elk's Jamboree Show...My N.C.O.'s...will agree that...I will be better employed with my natural talent...

If this meets with your approval...(please) forward my appllication to the proper authorities in Ottawa...

Respectfully...A.C. Bray

FROM: *Pilot Officer, J.R. Fisher*
         (for Director of Airmen Personnel Services)
TO: *Commanding Officer No. 16 S.F.T.S.,*
         Hagersville, Ontario
13 JANUARY 1943
    R160856 A.C. l. Bray
    The Director of Personnel Services advise that the services of the subject Airman are not required for the entertainment branch at this time. Please.
                    Signed Pilot Officer J.R. Fisher

THE AIRMAN (Official 'organ' of No. 3 "M" Depot, Edmonton, Canada
14 MAY 1943
BLACKOUTS OF '43 BEST YET!
    All Star RCAF Cast Features Beautiful W.D.'s ...in the arena last night...undoubtedly...was the best production ever to hit Edmonton...bar none!...LAC Mickey Horner played a terrific trumpet...brought more cries...Nice imitation of Clyde McCoy...Show was under the direction of F/O Wishart Campbell. Sound effects etc were superbly handled by...Cpl Terry Dowding...

MAJOR BOWES AMATEUR HOUR, C.B.S. Radio Theatre, 1697 Broadway, New York to Squadron Leader Norman Gilchrist...Director of Music. RCAF Ottawa, Ontario, Canada.
    16 MAY 1943
    ...our proposed series of three Major Bowes' broadcasts in Canada. We will do one Broadcast in Montreal and two in Ottawa...or two in Montreal and one in Ottawa...
                    Signed A.D. Rittenburg
                    MAJOR BOWES' AMATEUR HOUR

MAJOR BOWES' AMATEUR HOUR, C.B.S. Radio, New York
Squadron Leader N.M. Gilchrist, R.C.A.F.
23 DECEMBER 1943
Winners in the Final Audition Show
...the writer is sending you...the sum of $236.40...for round trip railroad fare...($24.28)...between Ottawa and New York...plus $3.00 for rations...for each of the five persons selected for the trip...

Prize winners included...AC1 Sam Levine and AC2 Neil Chotem
Six winners included AC2 Ellis McLintock, AC2 Hyman Goodman.
AW1 Honor Benson...

METROPOLITAN BROADCASTING SERVICES LIMITED
21 Dundas Square, Toronto, Ontario
    F/L G.B. Hislop, Recruiting Centre RCAF, Bay St., Toronto
    As I pointed out to you...there is considerable amount of excellent talent in the RCAF...Since starting the RCAF Tour for Talent broadcasts...I have unearthed enough talent to make up...two first rate road shows...It should be borne in mind that with exception of a few professionals...few of this vast potential talent...have any degree of stage presence...I believe...that consideration be taken...for 'crowd pleasers' rather than 'star'...
                    Signed Ken Soble

MEETING HELD IN OFFICE OF VICE MARSHALL J.A. SULLY
21 MAY 1943
    Discussions:...stressed...situation of Canadians overseas...long way from home...without entertainment...plan to have three (RCAF) shows throughout Canada and U.K...

MEMORANDUM
PG2/L Gilchrist, RCAF
7 AUGUST 1943
    A.M.P. desires that No. 1 Entertainment Group (Blackouts) proceed overseas as soon as possible...
    ...On their way East...it must be remembered they are to play...isolated prairie stations such as Mossbank etc...
                    Signed D.E. Kell, G.C.

ROYAL CANADIAN AIR FORCE
Official Report, No. 1 Unit, Western Tour

18 AUGUST 1943
    It is suggested that smaller units...be the aim of future entertainment in operational Commands...Since the "Blackouts" tour...noticable improvements have been

made...however, a show of this size cannot be easily managed...

...from a health standpoint alone it is felt that ventilation of recreation halls is a highly important factor...

...criticism was voiced concerning official publicity...acceptance of the show depends entirely on the picture and posters *designed by the Air Force Headquarters*...they were far from flattering...and inferior...Most commanding officers said that posters could be considered a misrepresentation...It is suggested that in future...accommodation for the Air Women be more carefully considered...

...it has been found that...the issue kit bag is definitely not the thing for standard use in travelling...

...difficulties of constant travel...increased through lack of laundry facilities...provision that at all times personnel meet the requirement of dress...

...(RCAF)...It is felt that entertainment has been long neglected item in the RCAF...continuation of official RCAF shows will find increasing success over anything that might be organized outside the service...*ONLY HERE IS THE TRUE APPRECIATION OF THE SERVICE MAN'S LIFE AND CONTRIBUTION TO HIS COUNTRY DEPICTED.*

Signed W.N.M. Campbell, O/C/No. 1, RCAF

MEMORANDUM RCAF "ALL CLEAR"
27 AUGUST 1943

...it is suggested that "THE BLACKOUTS OF 1943" be posted to RCAF Overseas Headquarters...

MEMORANDUM   RCAF
28 AUGUST 1943
ESTABLISHMENT FOR ADMINISTRATIVE OFFICER
for No. 2 Entertainment Group

The selection for the proper type of officer to fill the reference establishment has been under...consideration...that the individual designated must have certain special qualifications...

...unless the officer is an active participant in the show...it is...desirable that he possess a *keen interest in show business*...that he must...*mix with the cast in a friendly way* and yet maintain the dignity of his commissioned rank and authority...

...*must be categorized as a single man*...so that no separation from home...will interfere with his Services and duties...*he must also be able to keep his relationship with the W.D.'s (Air Women) on strictly an impersonal basis*...He must also *possess confidence and the ability to make friends easily* upon short notice...

THE MOST LIKELY CANDIDATE WAS FOUND...FLYING OFFICER A.A. MARSHALL of No. 11 Recruiting Centre, Toronto.

...He will assume his new duties end of September...

DIRECTORATE OF PUBLIC RELATIONS
For release in morning papers of September 8, 1943. Please guard against premature publication

8 SEPTEMBER 1943

"BLACKOUTS", the first R.C.A.F. all service musical show has now played to approximately 70,000 members of the Army, Navy and Air Force, during its five month tour.

It was on 'bush' stations, F/L Coote, director of the show, said that such welcomes were given as would gladden the heart of any troupe...A desert Harem number...featuring pretty women from the W.D.'s brought delighted "coos" from the friendly audiences...

...one uniformed stalwart, who had made a rough boat trip from a nearby 'bush' base...said..."This was worth getting seasick over." To which his friends chorused with gusto..."That it was! That it was!"

16 SEPTEMBER 1943

The second official Air Force show "ALL CLEAR" is being presented to RCAF personnel at the Red Triangle Club (Ottawa)...

...a third group will be formed in the near future...Live entertainment is a most important factor in respect to the continuance of high espirit de corps amongst (RCAF)...throughout Canada and Overseas...

(J.A. Sully) Air Vice Marshall

MEMORANDUM   No. 2 Entertainment Group RCAF
"ALL CLEAR"
20 SEPTEMBER 1943

Due to the confusion that has...existed during the final rehearsals...of "ALL CLEAR" certain names were submitted to your Directorate to be posted...etc...this action (now) should not have been taken and...individuals involved be retained...for the 3rd Entertainment Group to be know as "FLYING HIGH."

Signed, D.E. MacKell, G/C D of P

21 SEPTEMBER 1943

I enjoyed the presentation of the second official Air Force Show, "ALL CLEAR" very much. If there is any criticism, it might be that the orchestra tend to be a bit *too vigorous* and steal the show at times...

A. Ferrier, Air Vice Marshall, A.M.A.E.
*...I agree with that...(J.A. Sully, Air Vice Marshall)

NORWEGIAN CANADIAN PACKERS LTD. (Army, Navy Canteen Mess and Restaurant Contractors)
437 S. James St., West, Montreal
24 SEPTEMBER 1943
Squadron Leader N. Gilchrist, RCAF

I have now seen the enclosed regarding the RCAF show. It might be of interest for you to have before you some data on my son...

Someone was telling me that the RCAF required pigeons...I could let you have some 20 or 30 if these were any use...

Signed, Hugh A. Green

MEMORANDUM   ROYAL CANADIAN AIR FORCE
19 OCTOBER 1943
No. 1 Entertainment Group *BLACKOUTS*...re R165095
A/Cpl Levine S.R.

The subject N.C.O. is considered o be a very accomplished musician as regards to dance and theatrical band work...

...his enthusiasm and sincere interest in "*BLACKOUTS*" were responsible for most successful scenes, songs and routines...

...his is a good trouper...

...it is requested, please, that his recent promotion to the rank of '*Acting Corporal*' be authorized and that no action be taken to revert him to his previous rank...

Signed, D.E. MacKell, G/C D of P

CANADIAN JOINT STAFF, WASHINGTON
From Air Marshal L.S. Breadner, CB DSO, Chief of Air Staff, Ottawa
23 OCTOBER 1943

This is a note to let you know how well the No. 2 Entertainment Group (All Clear) has been received...in this vicinity...*They are definitely putting the RCAF on the map* with respect to the fact *that such a service exists.*

My idea was to invite as many...of the U.S., Army Navy, British and Dominion etc...

...I asked the *Minister* (?) if he would attend...however he took the view that it would be a most *dangerous* thing to do as it might lead to criticism...I pointed out to him...no charge would be made...

...I dropped the idea completely although Pearson or Mahony could see that any possible criticism...could arise...

I approached the Commanding Officer at Bolling Field (U.S.A.)...and he made available...seats for guests and Canadians...35 officers of Brigadier rank and up alone...attended...

I gave a dinner for Field Marshall, Sir John Dill, General Arnold, and Air Marshall Welsh...Admiral Sir Percy Noble would have been there but his wife was ill...General Giles, U.S. Chief of Staff also came...

The show was quite a success...and Gen. Arnold and Field Marshall Dill...visited the performers after the show to congratulate them...Flight Lieutenant Coote has done a splendid job...here...and the visit has been worthwhile...it is really something (Canadian) to be proud of...

Signed, Air Marshall Breadner

CANADIAN BROADCASTING CORPORATION Chester Bloom
24 OCTOBER 1943

It's a pity that every Canadian couldn't have heard the thrilling reception given here (Washington) by American audience...to the RCAF...show..."ALL CLEAR"...

I...attended the Friday night performance at Bolling Field...pack-jammed (jam packed) by more than 2,000 young flying men American and Canadian...civilians...and top ranking brass hats...

...Gen. (Hap) Arnold, sitting side by side with our Air Vice Marshall Welsh...

Generals, colonels, captains etc. of both nations...sat with representatives of our Canadian Legation...rocked the halls with laughter...

I'm not going to tell you about the merits of this entertaining show...hope many of you will see it in thefuture...spirit of...friendship...overflowed...between Canadians and Americans...

When people play together all the petty ill feelings engendered by selfish politicians are blown out the window on gales of laughter but our American cousins are sometimes inclined to forget we are British too...

Signed, Chester Bloom, C.B.C.

MEMORANDUM   RCAF Victory Loan Rally, Massey Hall, Toronto
26 OCTOBER 1943

It is requested...that the following airmen be authorized to proceed...in order to participate in the above noted rally.

R.67095   Sgt K. Bray
R.165960   Cpl. E.R. Horner

Sgt Bray is musical arranged and it is necessary he be available to work with the Army Band and Orchestra...

Cpl Horner...is a featured cornet soloist...

MEMORANDUM   RCAF 250-2-10
6 DECEMBER 1943
DAPS att. S/L Campbell, Entertainment Group #2, "ALL CLEAR"

...the nominal roll of No. 2 Entertainment Group, "ALL CLEAR" (included: Hyman Goodman: Weisbord; Kostenuk: Russo: M. Young (later the wife of Bill Kostenuk) etc...

OTTAWA, ONTARIO
13 DECEMBER 1943

No. 2 Entertainment Group "ALL CLEAR" will report to your H.Q. (Halifax) 30 December 1943...this show has been designed to entertain... airmen and airwomen...

...will travel...as a professional theatrical party...messing and quartering...The 9 airwomen in the party must be provided with special quarters...etc...Travel by train...will allow for proper berths...so that health be not impaired...

No member of the cast, with exception of officers are to be entertained in any officers' mess

...as the show will not arrive in time for regular meals...extra messing be provided...sandwiches and coffee...provided after each performance...soft drinks available during performance...

ROYAL CANADIAN AIR FORCE   Overseas Headquarters
The Secretary Dept. of National Defence for Air.
24 DECEMBER 1943

BLACKOUTS 1943, Overseas.

The Company performed very successfully during the voyage giving three two hour shows daily.

Blackouts arrived in London(England) 1300 hours Dec 8th 1943...men at Knights of Columbus and the women (W.D.'s) at the Y.W.C.A.

13 DECEMBER 1943

Premier performance at Comedy Theatre to a full house...Air Marshall Edwards, Air Marshall Breadner...visited the company back stage...

The Company have been very active...and except for a minor cold ailment and a sprained ankle have stood up remarkable well. The general worry at the moment is cold sleeping quarters and supplies of woollies and dressing gowns etc...

REPORT
Secretary, Dept. of National Defence
Ottawa
5 JANUARY 1944
No. 2 Entertainment units "ALL CLEAR"
Re. W.311126 A.W.2 Young, M.
R.143995 LAC Kostenuk, W.M.

The above couple were married during the Christmas Leave. They were A.W.O.L. (Absent Without Leave) 48 hours on Sunday, January 2, 1944...I advised other members...to locate the Kostenuks and tell them to report back...immediately. About 1400 hours, Kostenuk telephoned me and, after telling him that both he and his wife would be punished...he asked to be allowed to stay away until Monday...which, of course, I refused...they disobeyed my order and did not return until Monday, then being 72 hours

A.W.O.L...
In order to maintain discipline and my prestige...it is imperative that the couple be separated...as far as their RCAF duties are concerned...
Young, can be replaced easier than Kostenuk...
                    Signed, A.A. Marshall, F/O

MEMORANDUM   Royal Canadian Air Force
Entertainment Groups Overseas
6 JANUARY 1944   D.P.R. (Department of Public Relations)
    I am writing D.P.R. Overseas asking...that Blackouts 1943 be now called...Blackouts...It was presumed that D.P.R. would have automatically dropped '1943'...(It is now 1944)...review by *WINGS ABROAD...Headline "Blackouts Score Success in First Show"...is definitely favourable...*
    What criticism there is...is the privilege of a theatrical critic to be frank...
    When criticism contains a note of criticism...it does two things...actually whets the interest of the reader...inspires confidence of the reader in the critics honestly...WINGS ABROAD...operated by Service personnel...of D.P.R. overseas is not financed by Government Funds...it is a newspaper for the troops by the troops...
    Signed, G.M. Brown, D.P.R.

ROYAL CANADIAN AIR FORCE Overseas Headquarters, 13-12-4
SECRET   Attention of D.P. Ottawa, Ontario
Report on RCAF Entertainment Unit..."*BLACKOUTS*"
7 JANUARY 1944
    27.12.43 Departed London 1000 hours...arrived Chivener...2200 hours...(9 hours)...185 miles...(average 20.5 mph)...the drivers lost the way...Upon arrival...the trucks transporting equipment were missing...found later broken down at Bristol...
    Wing Commander Ashman, C.O. 407 Squadron, kindly vacated his home for the girls...(of the show)
    2.1.44 Played Regent Theatre to capacity of...4000 people...
    7.1.44 Tour ended.

    The company have done an excellent job but are showing sings of fatigue.

MEMORANDUM   AMP/D of P
10 JANUARY 1944
    "*BLACKOUTS*"...Reception overseas.
    ...it was possible to engage the Comedy Theatre (London) for Sunday and Monday...I had seen the show before but felt the London opening...was smoother and more finished...
    "Have never seen anything like it!" "This beats anything ENSA or the USA (American) people have produced" "This show is the tops!" were expressions used...
    ...the House Manager...stated..."This is the best show of its type ever to play this theatre..."
    ...I learned that the group (Blackouts)had some worried moments because of the non-arrival of stage props...and also because of the ignorance of English restaurant customs on Sundays...most of them do not open until after 7:00 p.m. ...the cast subsisted all day on a few sandwiches...
    A.A. McDermott, F/L Radio Liaison Off.

MEMORANDUM Royal Canadian Air Force
250-2-11
Entertainment No. 3 Training Command (Canada)
20 JANUARY 1944
    ...a party of 7 entertainers and three bandsmen is proceeding to #4 AGTS, Valleyfield...
    ...in as much as *these individuals* reflect the discipline and bearing of Air Force personnel, *please*, it is requested that these ten airmen be authorized to draw new uniform...*blue*...
                    J.A. Sully, Air Vice Marshall
    (**hand written note on official*
    MEMORANDUM...
    DDSA...Oh, to be an entertainer!...Phone SEO Rockcliffe and authorize him to relax period of wear somewhat, using his own common sense...Where..uniforms are perfectly serviceable, no *new issue* to be made...Signed, DSA.)

MEMORANDUM Royal Canadian Air Force
1 FEBRUARY 1944
Basic Training Entertainers
    W316656   Cpl Canty A.M.
    W318338   AW 2 Helwig, K.
    The two entertainers (above) will perform with the new All Girl Unit...now being assembled at Rockcliffe...Cpl Canty will be the star...and AW

2 Helwig...an important role.
...please...limit the basic training to 3 weeks rather than 5.

J.F. Coate S/L

HEADQUARTERS NEWFOUNDLAND BASE COMMAND, UNITED STATES ARMY
To Air Vice Marshall F.V. Heakes
2 FEBRUARY 1944

May I take this opportunity to express my appreciation...and of the entire garrison of Fort pepperell, for...your splendid show (RCAF) *ALL CLEAR*...I believe your method of handling this form of entertainment is far superior to ours, wherein we are furnished with USA troops composed of civilians whose performance...is not even mediocre...

John B. Brooks
Major General, Commanding U.S.Army

MEMORANDUM Royal Canadian Air Force
Report on *BLUES ON PARADE*
2 MARCH 1944

...this unit has not sufficient versatility in its personnel to do...a show...
The dance band is fairly adequate...
...a serious situation exists in the matter of morale of this unit...existing conflicts of personalities which render it impossible to function in harmony...
The pianist Cpl Corbett, is in very bad condition physically and mentally...the unit should be redistributed...

A.F. Lister, F.O. Entertainment.

(*Note on document...'action taken to disband this unit...')

TOUR OF THE "ALL CLEAR" R.C.A.F. SHOW Goose Bay
6 MARCH 1944 TO 3 MAY 1944

Dance...350 airmen attended and the only girls were from the Show...next dance for N.C.O.'s...again the only girls were from the show...This took up two evenings of the show but the station considered it *good for the morale*...
RCAF Summerside...recommend that no further shows be sent to this station...During our absence at Mount Pleasant, the airmens' quarters were turned into a shamble...bunks being dismantled and bedding covered with mud...The equipment officer S/L Roy refused to supply

(us) with bedding...
R.A.F. Greenwood...In spite of this station being advised...no one was prepared for our arrival...we waited at the station for 30 minutes for transportation and were taken in open stake trucks in the rain...P/O de Wolf was difficult to work with and (wanted) to operate the show his way...Would recommend no further shows be sent to above area...Our men had been quartered in a Seamens' Hotel and the place not only a dump but the washrooms were so filthy the men were forbidden to use them...
Major Nesbitt is responsible and he is most incompetent to handle an RCAF unit of any kind...
Personnel played to   143,000
Number of shows   135

A.A. Marshall F/O O.C.

MEMORANDUM Royal Canadian Air Force
THE MINISTER   Ottawa, Canada
13 APRIL 1944

In view of the glowing reports of the...success of the show "BLACKOUTS"...an ALL GIRL show was organized and especially equipped for performance overseas...The show was designed on the basis of experience gained in the U.K. where conditions are *vastly different* from those in Canada...
Unit consists of 1 W.D. Officer and 14 Other Ranks.
It is strongly recommended in view...that the ALL GIRL REVUE, known as *"W. DEBS* be assigned on overseas duty.

Robert Leckie, Air Marshall, Chief of Staff

ROYAL CANADIAN AIR FORCE   Overseas H.Q.
London, England
SECRET
1 JUNE 1944

The Secretary Dept. of Nat. Defence, Ottawa, Canada
     25.4.44 *BLACKOUTS*...7th Tour...
Proceeded to RAF Station Wrexham...It is not possible to present the show at this station had made arrangements for *movie*...
LAC HUNTER and LAW RENNIE were married with the approval of the undersigned and LAW Rennies *parents*...They had been engaged for the past eight months...

ROYAL CANADIAN AIR FORCE   250-14-2
CONFIDENTIAL
The Secretary Dept. of National Defence for Air, Ottawa
26 JUNE 1944

> Promotions: R141041 T.Sgt. Burgess, AA
> R211213 T.Cpl Gray A.N.
> R105878 LAW Weaver, R.F.
> *Records of the above personnel disclose that they are not qualified in drill.*
>
> S.A. Sprange, W/C Rockcliffe, Ontario

RCAF MESSAGE
8 JULY 1944

> Personnel of "BLACKOUTS" and "W.DEBS" companies total 51 to which you have..."TARMACS"...sent from here (Canada)..."ALL CLEAR" is being equipped for...overseas early August...Can also post "SWINGTIME" unit of 8 males for front line...
>
> C.G. Power Min. Nat. Defence

RCAF MESSAGE
22 JULY 1944

> ...break down "BLACKOUTS" into small groups...shows excellent...no need to return to Canada for re-equipping...E.N.S.A. sources have sufficient..."W DEBS" (all girl) very successful...but with "ALL CLEAR"...too large for transport...
> DANCE BANDS NEEDED...two small bands of 6 to 8 preferable to one large unit...With our large turnover of personnel...new faces and new shows...not important...
>
> Breadner, Air Vice Marshall

R.C.A.F. CONCERT PARTIES 1944
To Edgar Burton   Ottawa, 14 AUGUST 1944
General Manager
Robert Simpson Company, Toronto, Canada

> The RCAF show "ALL CLEAR" has just arrive in United Kingdom...due to demand it could not be presented in Canada prior to departure... May I express...our most sincere appreciation of your gracious donation of the costumes for this unit...
>
> Signed, J.A. Sully, Air Vice Marshall

(An American View)
HEADQUARTERS 1383 D AAF(American Air Force)
Base Unit
Presque Isle, Maine

26 AUGUST 1944
To: S/L/N. Gilchrist. Director of Music RCAF, Ottawa

> This headquarters desires to commend the *RCAF Concert Trio* for three splendid performances for the *AMERICAN personnel* of this base... ...musicianship of the trio was of a high calibre and was...very much enjoyed by three large audiences...Special commendation to Messrs *PHILIP PUCHTIAR, GLEAN GEARY AND COLIN BRAY* for their artistry...Their willingness to cooperate...for the benefit of the AMERICAN personnel of Labrador...is gratefully acknowledged...
>
> Signed, B.R. Hassell Lt/Col
> Commanding

(A Canadian View)
AIR OFFICER COMMANDING...HALIFAX
RCAF Entertainment Unit
28 AUGUST 1944

> The...unit, consisting of *LAC BRAY C.M.R., LAC PUCHTIAR, P.D. and LAC GEARY, G.W.* a pianist, violinist and vocalist, which visited this station...was much appreciated...
> Three performances were given but a fourth...was cancelled...since it was considered there would be not sufficient attendance...for this fine trio... While the presentation was excellent, it is felt that the artists *be furnished with blazers and flannel trousers,* or some more appropriate form of attire than the RCAF uniform...This (uniform) *was designed for service use but* not for artistic presentations... it is proposed that airmen be afforded an opportunity... for...more attractive dress...
>
> J.F. Grant, S/L Yarmouth, NS

RCAF MESSAGE to Minister
21 SEPTEMBER 1944

> Imperative send trumpet player as requested for "ALL CLEAR" Party...

29 SEPTEMBER 1944   Reply from Ottawa

> Trumpet player LAC G.R. Allen proceeding first convenient date.

2 NOVEMBER 1944 From RCAF England

> Trumpeter for "ALL CLEAR" arrived...Please send trumpet...

REVISED ITINERARY FOR MASSEY HARRIS "COMBINES"
6 DECEMBER 1944

> Party consisting of 24 people (10 men and 14

women), all members of the Massey Harris Company Limited.

For use in the RCAF training command.

Signed J.A. Sully, Air Vice Marshall

ROYAL CANADIAN AIR FORCE
Attn: S/L N.M. Gilchrist

Entertainment Report
21 DECEMBER 1944
Completed tour of Whitehorse
...not feasible to use station personnel in these area due to: lack of talent, no pianist, vocalists, dancers, instrumentalists, inadequate facilities, small numbers of station personnel...mostly on shift work, no W.D.'s (Women) and general lack of interest...

The need for entertainment along this route is desperate...the Americans are able to send shows regularly...but nothing from our own RCAF...

H. Singer, F/Sgt

ITINERARY OF RCAF MODERNAIRES DANCE BAND
NO.3 RCAF
23 JUNE TO 29 JUNE 1945
Included such:
Item #13   On June 28th band will play 'chamber music' during afternoon Garden Fete in Peterborough, England
Item #19   The attention of S/L Boundy and the leader of the dance band is especially drawn to Item #13...
The words 'chamber music' may be incorrectly used. The band will be expected to play numbers to entertain visitors at the fete and will not be...dance numbers.

ROYAL CANADIAN AIR FORCE, Overseas
The Secretary Dept. of National Defence, Ottawa
27 NOVEMBER 1945
Entertainment Sections
...the health of the entertainment personnel has been a matter of concern...particularly the W.D.'s (Women) In some cases the Medical Officers...prescribed they should not go on the road again...

After Jan 1st 1946...it can no longer be maintained...The health of the personnel being left overseas is being affected.

H.B. Godwin, Air Commodore

R.C.A.F. ENTERTAINMENT OVERSEAS
7 DECEMBER 1945
From W/C N.M. Gilchrist
...there are no entertainers now in Service in Canada. The establishment has been deleted... Your request for overseas replacements cannot be met.